Leadership Lessons From

The Son Of

A Terrible Golfer

Stenette Byrd III, Ed.D.
&
Stenette Byrd IV

Library of Congress Control Number: 2025927324

ISBN Number: 979-8-9933588-2-6

For inquiries and details, contact the publisher at
info@thirdforcesolutions.com

Dedication

This book is dedicated to seasoned and aspiring leaders and golfers. Leadership and golf are both games of precision, patience, and the courage to admit when you're in the rough. This journey is for anyone who knows that preparation and persistence is the only way to beat the odds and master the scorecard.

Enjoy!

Stenette & Stenette

Table of Contents

THIRD FORCE
EDUCATIONAL SOLUTIONS LLC

Abstract

My dad is a lot of things. A great leader. An inspiring speaker. A fierce advocate for kids. But a good golfer? Not so much. My dad has a handicap of 20. For those who don't know, that means he's probably going to hit somewhere around 92 to 95 strokes on a good day. Breaking 90 is a rare, almost mythical event for him. For my friends and me, it's just another Saturday.

Growing up in Suffolk, Virginia, I had the luxury of playing at some great courses. I was the captain of my high school golf team, and I was pretty good. I was also the captain of my soccer team and my eSports team. I learned that being a good leader meant you had to know the rules of the game. My dad, on the other hand, made his own rules on the course.

"Son," he would often say, "I'm not playing against the other guys, I'm playing against the course."

I get the logic, but that doesn't explain why he keeps trying to hit a 3-wood from a hundred yards out of the rough. The man is a math whiz, but his on-course calculations are a tragedy. It's like he sees a straight line from tee to hole, ignoring all the trees, water hazards, and bunkers in between. I always tell him, "Dad, you have to play the course as it is, not as you want it to be."

This is where the real fun begins. I'll give him a simple tip, something about club selection or a smoother swing, and he'll nod his head and then launch into a full-blown leadership lecture. He'll say something like, "Ivy (this is the nickname my parents gave me), that's what a good leader does. They don't just see the problem; they see the pathway to the solution. They don't try to force a shot they don't have; they play the ball where it lies and focus on the next shot."

I've heard these lectures on the first tee, in the fairway, and in the sand trap. He says the golf course is a microcosm of leadership, where every shot is a decision, and every hole is a new challenge. He says you can't be a great leader without a healthy dose of humility, and you can't improve your golf game without acknowledging your weaknesses.

I still don't understand why he doesn't just use an 8-iron from the fairway, but I've started to see his point. He's not just playing a game; he's working through a problem. Every bad shot is a chance to learn, and every good shot is a small victory.

He's a terrible golfer, but he's a great leader. And maybe, just maybe, the two are more connected than I ever thought. What do you think?

— Stenette "Ivy" Byrd IV

Glossary Of Golf Terms Used Throughout This Book

- **18 holes:** A full round of golf. It's the standard length of a professional or recreational game. It's the full experience. You'll hear golfers say, "let's play a full 18" when they want to play a complete game.
- **Back Nine:** The final nine holes of an 18-hole golf course (holes 10-18). It's the stretch where you either hold it all together or let the wheels fall off.
- **Birdie:** A score of one stroke less than par on a single hole. For example, on a Par 4, if you take 3 shots (which is one better than expected), you have made a birdie.
- **Bogey:** A score of one stroke over par on a single hole. For example, on a Par 4, if you take 5 shots, you have made a bogey.
- **Bunker:** A hazard on the golf course that is a prepared area of ground, often a hollow, from which turf or soil has been removed and replaced with sand or the like.
- **Chip:** A short, low-lofted shot, usually played close to the green. It is a shot designed to get the ball onto the green and rolling toward the hole.
- **Dogleg:** A golf hole that bends to the left or right, presenting a strategic challenge for the golfer.
- **Double bogey:** A score of two strokes over par on a single hole. On a Par 4, if you take 6 shots, you've made a double bogey.

- **Fairway:** The part of the golf hole between the tee box and the green. The grass is cut short, making it the ideal surface for your next shot. You always want to be in the fairway because it gives you the best lie to hit your next shot.
- **Front Nine:** The first nine holes of an 18-hole golf course (holes 1-9). This is where you set the tone for your round, a lot like the first day of school.
- **Green:** The area of specially prepared grass at the end of a golf hole, where the cup is located. It is the final destination for each hole.
- **Handicap:** A numerical measure of a golfer's ability, used to create fair competition between players of different skill levels. For example, if I shoot an average score of 85, but my dad's average score is 100, he would win the round if I am unable to keep my score 15 points less than his. For the purpose of this book, my dad's golf handicap of 20 means that he usually takes 20-25 additional shots than expected, for the course he is playing.
- **Hazard:** An obstacle on a golf course, such as a bunker, water, marsh or a ravine. When your ball lands in a hazard, there's usually a penalty, or it can be a challenge to get your ball out of the area.
- **Lie:** This refers to the position of the ball when it comes to rest on the ground. A good lie is when the ball sits up nicely on the grass, giving you a clean shot. A bad lie is when the ball is sitting down in the thick grass, a divot, or a hole.
- **Mulligan:** A do-over. It's an unofficial rule where you get to retake a shot without penalty. Most golfers use a mulligan on the first tee box. They aren't legal in tournaments.

- **Par:** The standard number of strokes a golfer is expected to take to complete a single hole or a full 18-hole round. For example, a hole that is a Par 4 means a skilled golfer is expected to get the ball in the hole in four shots. Most 18-hole golf courses have a Par of 72.
- **Putt:** A shot played with a putter on the green to roll the ball into the hole.
- **Sand trap:** Another name for a bunker. You'll often hear golfers use these terms interchangeably.
- **Tee box:** The designated area at the beginning of each hole where golfers take their first shot. You can use a tee to prop your ball up to hit it with a driver.
- **The Turn:** The halfway point in a round of golf, typically between the 9th and 10th holes. This is a great time to reflect on your round so far and prepare for the next nine holes.
- **Triple bogey:** A score of three strokes over par on a single hole. As a terrible golfer, this is my dad's favorite term. A triple bogey on a Par 4 means you've taken 7 shots.

Introduction

If you read my dad's first book, *Leadership Lessons from a Terrible Golfer*, you are already familiar with the central paradox of the Byrd household. You know that my father is an incredible leader who can analyze complex data, rally a school staff, and turn a culture around with the precision of a mathematician. You also know that he is a tragic golfer. If there is a tree on the course, he will find it; if there is water, his ball has a homing device for it. While he excels as an educational leader, his journey to break 90 has been a long, winding road that we have walked together.

My name is Stenette Byrd IV, around the clubhouse, I'm known as Ivy, the guy trying to fix his dad's swing. At the time of writing this, I am a freshman at Norfolk State University (Behold the Green and Gold). Before heading to college, I spent my high school years as the captain of both the varsity soccer and golf teams. I have spent thousands of hours on the range studying the mechanics of the swing, course management, and the mental resilience required to play this game well. I've watched my dad try to apply his strict logic and grit to the sport, often with mixed results, and I've realized that while I was teaching him how to read a green, he was teaching me how to read people.

Let's be honest about something up front: I generally do not enjoy reading long, dense books. Between my college classes, labs, and social life, I don't have the time or patience to wade through three hundred pages of theory just to get to the point. I suspect that as busy leaders and/or students, you probably feel the same way. That is why we designed this book to be different. It is built to be light, practical, and efficient; mimicking the flow of a perfect round of golf.

We have structured the book into eighteen easy-to-read chapters, with each chapter representing a specific hole on one of our favorite local courses. In every chapter, I will start by breaking down the hole from a golfer's perspective, highlighting the hazards, the layout, and the best strategy to attack the pin. Then, my dad will take over, translating that specific golf scenario into a practical application for leadership. Whether it is navigating a dogleg left or recovering from a bunker, we are going to show you how the strategy on the course mirrors the leadership strategies in every organization. So, grab your clubs and your notebook; we are on the first tee.

— **Stenette "Ivy" Byrd IV**

The Course Map & Score Card

Here is the 'Course Map.' Column 2 outlines the unique features of our favorite holes, while Column 3 lists the leadership attributes essential for organizational success. Before you begin the book, please use the Pre-Assessment in Column 4 to rate yourself on each of these 18 attributes. You will find the same chart at the end of the book for you to track your growth.

The Scorecard (Pre-Assessment): 18 Holes, 18 Lessons

1 - I have mastered this skill

2 - I'm pretty good in this area

3 - I want to be better in this area

4 - I really struggle in this area

5 - I have no idea why this is important

Hole	Chapter Title	The Leadership Attribute	Pre-Assessment Score
1	The Tee Box	Vision And Setting The Tone	
2	The Trap Of The Big Stick	Discipline And Restraint	
3	The Hidden Graveyard	Strategic Agility	
4	Out of the Pit And Into The Sand	Resilience And Grit	
5	The High Stakes Of The Hazzard	Risk Management	
6	Reading The Wind	Situational Awareness	
7	The Fine Print	Attention To Detail	

8	Trampolines And Territory	Patience And Endurance	
9	The Mentor And The Mentee	Mentoring And Mentorship	
10	Seizing Opportunities	Seizing Opportunities	
11	The Sidehill Lie	Balance And Stability	
12	Divots And Decisions	Accountability And Repairing Trust	
13	The High Stakes Of The Inner Circle	People Before Programs	
14	Finesse Over Force	Emotional Intelligence	
15	Playing It Where It Lies	Leading *Your* Organization	
16	Leading Within The White Stakes	Ethics And Boundaries	
17	The Five-Foot Foundation	Performance Under Pressure	
18	Choosing the Right Team Members	Choosing The Right Team Members	
		Total Pre-Assessment Score	

Hole # 1: The Tee Box

There is no feeling in sports quite like standing on the first tee box in the early morning. The dew is still on the grass, the mower is humming in the distance, and you have a completely blank scorecard. You are undefeated. I can see the look of hope in Dad's eyes because at this specific moment, we have the exact same score. Par is within reach. The birds are chirping as we settle into the seats of our golf cart at The Riverfront Golf Club in Suffolk, Virginia.

This place is home turf. I spent my high school years and summers working here, picking up balls from the range and parking carts. As we take off, we wave to James in the cart barn; he gives us a nod that implies he knows exactly how many balls we're about to lose.

We then drive up to Harves, the starter, who is the gatekeeper of the course and never misses a chance to roast us. He leans into the cart, looks at my dad, and shakes his head. "Dr. Byrd," he says with a straight face, "you have done a terrible job raising this son of yours. The boy needs to be taught some manners and respect."

We all burst out laughing as we ease off the brake. It's the perfect start to the day.

But the laughter stops about thirty yards later.

Directly in front of us is the blue tee box. To play from here, you have to launch the ball over a significant stretch of marshland. Dad stops the cart. He stares at the fairway beyond the marsh and puffs out his chest a little.

"I feel good today, Son," he says, gripping the steering wheel. "I think I can make it over."

I look at the marsh. I look at the brand-new sleeve of Titleist golf balls in the back of the golf cart.

"Dad," I say, keeping my voice calm. "You are looking at the Blue tees. There is absolutely no reason to risk starting your day in the mud. Let's go to the Whites."

He hesitates. He does the mental math. Finally, he nods. "You're right."

We turn the bend and arrive at the White tees. The view clears up, and we are looking down a beautiful landscape. It's a long Par 4, wide open, but visually intimidating. There is a deep sand trap waiting way down on the left side, just begging for a missed shot.

The marsh is behind us. The fairway is ahead of us.

"Okay," I say, handing him his driver. "Tee it up."

The Tee Box is unique for one reason: It is the only time in the entire round where you have 100% control over your ball placement (your lie). You get to choose where to stand between the markers. You get to tee the ball up as high or as low as you want. The ground is flat. There are no divots.

Most amateurs (like my dad) rush this moment. They just want to hit the "big stick" (the driver) and crush it. They walk up, plant their feet, and swing hard. But golf is a game of angles. If your feet are aimed into the woods, it doesn't matter how good your swing is, the ball is going into the woods.

The Strategy

- **Visualize:** Before you put the tee in the ground, stand behind the ball and pick a specific target. Not "the fairway." A specific tree branch or patch of grass.
- **Align:** Set your club face to that target first, then set your feet.
- **Check Tempo:** The first swing sets the rhythm for the day. Don't try to win the Masters on the first shot.

If you don't respect the setup, you'll spend the rest of the hole scrambling to save par.

The Leadership Lesson (Dad's Take)

My son "Ivy" is right about the angles. In geometry, if a line deviates by just one degree at the start, after travelling a long distance, it will be miles away from the objective.

In leadership, the Tee Box is the Launch. It's the first staff meeting of the school year. It's the kickoff of a new strategic plan. It's the first 90 days of a new job.

Many leaders make the same mistake high-handicap golfers make: They rush to action. They want to "hit the ball" (start the work) before they have established the aim. They mistake activity for achievement.

The "Old School" Truth: It is very difficult to recover from a bad start simply by working harder. If you launch a new initiative without clear alignment, your team will work incredibly hard to run in the wrong direction.

3 Ways to Tee Up Your Team For Success

Control the Environment: Just like the tee box is the only controlled lie, the "Launch" is the only time you fully control the message. Once your plan is activated, the whirlwind takes over (the wind, the rain, the bad bounces). Use your "Tee Box" time to be crystal clear about the Mission.

Aim Small, Miss Small: Don’t give your organization vague goals like "We want to be better." That’s like aiming at "the fairway." Give them a specific target: "We will increase 3rd-grade reading proficiency by 10%."

Check the Grip: Before you unleash the team, check the fundamentals. Are the resources in place? Is the culture ready? Don't swing until you are balanced.

The Takeaway: You can’t win the tournament on the first hole, but you can certainly lose it. Take your time. Set your feet. Aim true.

We’ve hit our drives. I’m in the middle of the fairway (obviously). And Dad... well, he’s in the short grass, so we’ll take it.

Summary: A Clean Start

The strategy paid off. I stuck my second shot on the green and two-putted for a routine par. Dad didn’t quite reach the green in regulation, his approach fell a little short, but he kept his head cool. A solid chip got him close, and he cleaned up for a respectable Bogey.

No lost balls. No water hazards. No marsh.

This clean start was only possible because we managed the biggest hazard on the course first: our egos. My dad wanted to hit from the Blues because he felt good, not because his average driving distance justified it. In golf, the tee box you choose dictates the difficulty of the entire round. Think of it like a difficulty setting in a video game.

The Blue Tees: Usually reserved for the best players who have the skill and power to play an extended version of the course.

The White Tees: The fair challenge. This is where the game is designed to be played for the average golfer.

The Forward Tees: These remove forced carries (like that marsh we just avoided).

If you play from a tee box that doesn't match your skill set, you aren't challenging yourself; you are punishing yourself. You force yourself to swing harder to clear obstacles that shouldn't even be in play, which destroys your tempo and ruins your mechanics.

The Bottom Line: Swallow your pride. Play the tees that allow you to reach the fairway in regulation. You'll have more fun, and honestly, nobody cares which color plastic marker you stood next to when you write a "4" on the scorecard.

Lastly, we have a good opening strategy: visualize, align and check tempo.

With a Par and a Bogey safely on the card, we throw the clubs back in the bag. We've survived the opener at The Riverfront, but for Hole 2, we're heading 7.3 miles to another one of our favorite local courses, also located in Suffolk, Virginia. But first, let's track our scores.

The Scorecard: Hole # 1: The Tee Box

Instructions:

Column 1 (The Date): This book is a living document. We don't expect you to master these lessons overnight. We want you to come back to this page and record the date as you track your growth in each area.

Column 2 (The Golfer): Use the key below to record how you handle playing from the appropriate tee box. This should be an easy one (pun intended)!

Column 3 (The Leader): Using the key below, record where you stand in your leadership journey as it relates to Vision and Setting the Tone.

1 - I have mastered this skill
2 - I'm pretty good in this area
3 - I want to be better in this area
4 - I really struggle in this area
5 - I have no idea why this is important

Hole #1 Date (M/D/Y)	**Golf Score** Willingness to play from the appropriate tee box	**Leadership Score** Vision and Setting the Tone
__/__/__		
__/__/__		
__/__/__		
__/__/__		

Hole # 2: The Trap Of The Big Stick

Alright, throw your bag on the cart. We are heading over to another one of our absolute favorite spots: Sleepy Hole Golf Course in Suffolk, Virginia.

Now, everyone talks about the finish at Sleepy Hole. The 18th is spectacular. It runs right along the Nansemond River, winds can be brutal but the view is unmatched. But you can't get to the glory of the 18th if you blow up your scorecard on the front nine. That brings us to Hole 2.

On paper, Hole 2 at Sleepy Hole Golf Course looks like an opportunity for an easy birdie. It's a Par 5. For the average "Terrible Golfer" (like my father), seeing "Par 5" triggers a common response: Grab the driver and swing out of your shoes.

Do not do that!

Hole 2 is a deception. It features an early, sharp dogleg left. It baits you into trying to cut the corner or overpower it. Here is the reality check:

The Long Mistake: If you hit the driver too well (accidentally or on purpose), you will run straight through the fairway and end up deep in the trees on the far side.

The Right Mistake: If you get nervous and push the ball to the right to avoid the dogleg, you are hitting into a thicket. You won't be looking for the green on your second shot; you'll be punching out sideways.

This hole isn't a test of power; it's a test of discipline.

The winning play here is boring, and I mean that in the best way possible. Leave the headcover on the driver. Take out a hybrid or a mid-iron. All you need is a shot that goes 140 to 160 yards, dead straight. That gets you to the elbow of the turn, opens up the entire fairway, and turns a potential double-bogey disaster into an easy three-shot path to the green.

Dad hates this advice because it doesn't feel "cool" to tee off with a 6-iron on a Par 5. But I'd rather be 160 yards down the middle than 250 yards into the woods.

"Dad, tell them why holding back is sometimes the strongest move you can make."

The Leadership Lesson (Dad's Take)

My son is right, even if it pains me to leave the driver in the bag.

There is something seductive about the "Big Stick." It feels powerful. It makes a loud noise. It looks impressive. But on Hole 2 at Sleepy Hole, the Big Stick is a liar. It promises distance but usually delivers disaster.

In leadership, discipline is often defined not by what you do, but by what you refuse to do.

When a leader enters a new organization or faces a crisis, "The Driver" represents your ultimate authority. It is the ability to fire people, to mandate immediate change, to rewrite policy overnight, or to say, "Do it because I said so."

Just like on the tee box, many young leaders (and impatient older ones) step up to a problem and immediately swing as hard as they can. They want to show strength. They want to make a statement.

But here is the truth about "The Driver" of Authority: If you use it recklessly, you will spend the rest of your time punching out of the woods.

The Discipline of Restraint

Restraint is the hardest skill to master because it feels like passivity. It isn't. It is calculated positioning.

When you walk into a school or a boardroom that requires a turnaround, you might see 50 things that need to be fixed. The undisciplined leader tries to fix all 50 in the first week (hitting the driver). The result? You alienate your staff, you break trust, and you create "organizational trees" that block your view of the goal.

The disciplined leader takes the "Iron off the tee."

You observe before you act (Check the yardage). You secure small wins before attempting massive overhauls (Hit the fairway). You position yourself for a successful second move (Set up the approach).

I have seen superintendents and CEOs blow up their tenure in the first 90 days because they tried to overpower the culture rather than navigate it. They ended up deep in the thicket, fighting just to get back to the fairway, while the disciplined leader was already on the green putting for birdie.

The Takeaway

Don't confuse restraint with weakness. It takes more strength to holster your power than it does to brandish it. On Hole 2, and in your organization, play the shot that keeps you in the game, not the one that strokes your ego.

The Summary

In golf, distance is an advantage, but only when accompanied by direction. On the deceptive 2nd hole at Sleepy Hole Golf Course, the desire to use maximum power is actually a trap that leads to the woods. The same is true in leadership. The most effective leaders possess the discipline to pause, assess the layout, and choose the path of least resistance rather than the path of greatest force. Restraint is not a lack of action; it is the strategic preservation of your position.

The Reflection

Look at a current challenge in your organization where you feel the urge to force a quick resolution or assert your authority loudly.

Ask yourself: If I use “The Driver" here (immediate mandates, firing, forced policy), where might I end up in the trees?

____

____

____

____

Then ask: What is the "6-Iron" approach: the smaller, safer step that keeps the team in the fairway and sets us up for an easier shot tomorrow?

____

____

____

____

Ivy's Related Golf Tip: "Tee It Low to Let It Go"

If you are taking my advice and hitting an iron or hybrid off the tee on a Par 5, do not tee the ball up as high as you would for a Par 3.

The Tip: Tee the ball low—almost level with the grass.

The Why: When you tee an iron too high, you risk hitting it high on the face, which balloons the ball into the wind and kills your distance. A lower tee encourages a solid, downward strike. You want a boring, piercing flight that hits the fairway and rolls. Save the high bombs for the driving range.

By trading power for position, Dad and I stayed in the hunt with a bogey and a par, respectively. Remember, the "Big Stick" might get the cheers, but disciplined club selection is what keeps your leadership strategy on the fairway.

Hole # 2 Scorecard: Restraint & Discipline

Instructions:

Column 1 (The Date): This book is a living document. We don't expect you to master these lessons overnight. We want you to come back to this page and record the date as you track your growth in each area.

Column 2 (The Golfer): Use the key below to record your willingness to put away the driver when a safe shot is the best option.

Column 3 (The Leader): Using the key below, record where you stand in your leadership journey as it relates to showing restraint and discipline.

Note: We hope that you have the idea of how to use the scorecard. As a result, this explanation will not be provided in future chapters.

1 - I have mastered this skill
2 - I'm pretty good in this area
3 - I want to be better in this area
4 - I really struggle in this area
5 - I have no idea why this is important

Hole #2 Date (M/D/Y)	**Golf Score** Willingness to avoid the driver on holes that require a safe first shot	**Leadership Score** Restraint & Discipline
__/__/__		
__/__/__		
__/__/__		
__/__/__		

Hole # 3: The Hidden Graveyard

Now let's hop in the cart and head 24 miles over to the third tee box at Kiln Creek Golf Course located in Newport News, Virginia. As we pull up, you'll notice my dad is already checking his yardage book and squinting at the GPS, convinced he can "solve" this Par 4. To the naked eye, this looks like a straightforward, beautiful fairway. It's the kind of view that gives you a boost of confidence, making you want to pull out the driver and let it rip right down the middle. It's an inviting stretch of green that seems to promise an easy path to the cup.

However, Hole 3 is a deceptive 340-yard Par 4. From the tee, the fairway looks wide and forgiving. But if you watch the guys who have played this course every Saturday for twenty years, they aren't aiming for the center. They are aiming way right, almost towards the tee box of the previous hole, which looks like a mistake to the uninitiated. They know something the yardage book doesn't emphasize: the terrain has a mind of its own.

Dad steps up to the ball with the visualization, alignment and proper tempo that we discussed back on hole 1. He swings hard and connects perfectly, sending a piercing drive right down the center of the fairway. "Ivy, look at that," he says, starting to walk back to the cart with a satisfied grin. "Center cut. Geometry doesn't lie." We drive down the path, but as we get closer to where the ball landed, the "geometry" of the earth reveals its secret. The fairway has a massive, hidden undulation—a crater that is completely invisible from the tee box. Even though his ball hit the dead center of the grass, the severe slope caught it and funneled it straight into a deep depression of grass and rocks. The ball has disappeared into a hidden graveyard where I suspect thousands of balls are hidden. Instead of a clean approach, like me, he has to take a drop where he's now standing in a deep crater, looking up at a green he can no longer see.

In golf, perception isn't always reality. A shot can look perfect in the air and still end up in a disaster because of the "unseen hazards" of the terrain. If Dad had listened when I told him to aim twenty yards further right than he thought necessary, he'd be sitting on flat ground with a clear look at the pin. This is the essence of the pivot. Strategic agility in golf is the ability to change your target based on the "intel" of the terrain and the wisdom of those who have walked it before, rather than just relying on how good your swing feels in the moment.

My dad goes on to explain.

This is a classic leadership trap. We often design amazing initiatives in the boardroom that look flawless on paper. From the "tee box" of the district office, the plan looks straight, logical, and destined for success. But your "locals;" the staff, and the frontline employees, know where the craters are. They know that even if the plan looks good, the underlying culture or the timing has a slope that will pull your initiative into the abyss. If your team tells you to "aim right," don't take it as a challenge to your authority; take it as vital data.

Strategic agility is the willingness to change your aim mid-stream when you realize the landscape isn't what you thought it was. A leader who refuses to pivot because "the plan was sound" will spend their whole career hitting out of craters. To lead effectively, you have to be willing to listen to the people who are actually standing on the ground where the ball is going to land. Don't let a "perfect" plan blind you to the reality of the terrain.

Before you tee off on an unfamiliar course, or launch a new organizational goal, always ask about "the miss." Knowing where not to hit it is often more important than knowing where you want it to go.

A Tip for the Golf Course and The Boardroom

As we move toward the green, take a second to reflect:

Who is a "local(s)" on your team who can help you avoid the graveyards?

____

____

Think back to your last major decision, then use the self-assessment tool below to capture your score on this hole.

Hole #3 Score Card: Strategic Agility

1 - I have mastered this skill
2 - I'm pretty good in this area
3 - I want to be better in this area
4 - I really struggle in this area
5 - I have no idea why this is important

Hole #3 Date (M/D/Y)	**Golf Score** Pivoting based on the terrain and advice from those who know the course better than you	**Leadership Score** Strategic Agility
__/__/__		
__/__/__		
__/__/__		
__/__/__		

Hole # 4: Out Of The Pit And Into The Sand

The aftermath of Hole 3 at Kiln Creek wasn't pretty. I walked away with a bogey after missing the green on my second shot; a mental error more than a physical one. Dad, however, had it much worse. He walked away with a double bogey, though it felt like a ten. He spent his third shot (after a penalty drop) just trying to climb out of that "graveyard" crater, and by the time he two-putted on the green, his "geometry" was looking more like the path our dog, Fibo (short for Fibonacci), takes to find the spot he wants poop. We hopped in the cart, shook it off, and made the drive over to Bid-A-Wee Golf Course, located in Portsmouth, Virginia (24.5 miles from Kiln Creek).

We pulled up to the 4th hole, a short, picturesque Par 3. It's the kind of hole that looks easy until you see the massive sand traps guarding the left side like hungry mouths. I stepped up with my 9-iron, caught it clean, and watched the ball dance toward the hole, settling just five feet away for an easy birdie look. Dad, still feeling the disappointment of the previous hole, swung for the fences. The ball took a sharp turn left, hit the lip of the bunker, and disappeared into the white sand. As we walked toward the green, I saw him staring into that pit, and I knew exactly what he was thinking. Believe it or not, this is actually a shot where my dad excels. We are going to share what we have learned through the years with you.

The Grit of the Bunker

Being in a bunker is the ultimate test of a golfer's temperament. It is the physical manifestation of a mistake. In the fairway, you have options;

in the sand, you have a problem. To get out, you can't be timid, and you can't be frantic. You need resilience, the ability to accept that you are in a bad spot, and grit, the determination to swing through the heavy resistance to find the green again.

Getting out of the sand requires a specific set of mechanics that mirror how a leader handles a crisis. Here are five tips from me and my dad for escaping the bunker and the leadership implications they carry:

Open Your Stance: In the sand, you have to aim slightly left and open the clubface to let the bounce of the club work.

Leadership Link: When you're in a "sandy" situation at work, you can't use the same standard approach. You have to open your mind to different perspectives and adjust your stance to see the problem from a new angle.

Don't Hit the Ball: You actually want to hit the sand about two inches behind the ball. The explosion of sand is what lifts the ball out.

Leadership Link: Sometimes, to solve a problem, you shouldn't attack the "ball" (the person or the direct symptom). You have to address the "sand" (the environment or the underlying cause) to get things moving again.

Commit to the Swing: If you decelerate in the sand, the ball stays in the pit. You have to accelerate through the resistance.

Leadership Link: In a crisis, half-measures fail. Once you decide on a recovery plan, you must lead with full commitment. Indecision or "slowing down" mid-pivot will leave your team stuck in the hole.

Follow Through: Your finish should be high and proud, even if the shot was ugly.

Leadership Link: Resilience is about finishing the task. Even if the recovery process is messy, a leader must see it through to the end to ensure the organization regains its momentum.

Leave the Sand Behind: Once you hit the shot, rake the bunker and move on.

Leadership Link: Don't carry the weight of the crisis into the next meeting. Once a problem is solved, learn the lesson, "rake the area" to leave it better for the next person, and focus on the next tee box.

The Turnaround

Dad took a deep breath, stepped into the sand, and remembered the "Old School" grit he's always preaching. He didn't try to be cute with it; he swung hard, splashed the sand, and watched his ball pop up and roll within ten feet of the cup. He didn't get the birdie, like me, but he saved the hole with a par. As we walked to the next tee, he looked at me and said, "Ivy, leadership isn't about avoiding the sand; it's about knowing how to get out when you land in it."

Practice Tips: The Recovery Drills

For the Golf Game: Go to the practice bunker and draw a line in the sand two inches behind a row of balls. Practice hitting that line every time. The goal isn't to hit the ball far; it's to get comfortable with the "thump" of the sand.

For the Leadership Game: Practice "Scenario Pivoting." During your next staff meeting, present a hypothetical "worst-case scenario" (a budget cut, a key resignation, a facility failure) and ask the team: "What is our move two inches behind the problem?" Identify the environmental factors you need to change to "lift" the organization out of the crisis.

Hole #4 Score Card: Resilience & Grit

1 - I have mastered this skill

2 - I'm pretty good in this area

3 - I want to be better in this area

4 - I really struggle in this area

5 - I have no idea why this is important

Hole #4 Date (M/D/Y)	**Golf Score** Playing out of the bunker	**Leadership Score** Resilience & Grit
__/__/__		
__/__/__		
__/__/__		
__/__/__		

Hole # 5: The High Stakes Of The Hazard

"Son, keep those sunglasses on. You're going to need them to see the trouble we're about to get into." I'm steering the cart over to the 5th tee box, at the Riverfront Golf Course back in Suffolk, and the vibe has shifted. We just finished Hole 4, talking about getting "Out of the Pit" and handling the sand, but now we're staring at a different kind of monster.

Dad stops the cart and points toward the horizon with a grimace. "Look at this, Ivy. We've got 160 yards of marsh and water just to reach the fairway. If I try to 'hero' this with a driver, I'm flirting with the marsh on the right or the tree and house on the left. This isn't just a golf hole; it's a Par 4 masterclass in Risk Management. You have to decide: are you playing for the highlight reel, or are you playing to stay in the game?"

From my perspective, Hole 5 at Riverfront is the ultimate "thinking man's" hole. From the tee box, you are staring at a forced carry. You have to clear that 160 yards of marsh just to find a blade of grass. Most people see the fairway in the distance and immediately want to grip it and rip it, but that's where the disaster starts. First, if you don't hit it pure, you're in the marsh for an immediate penalty. Second, even if you crush a driver, the fairway narrows significantly the further you go. You've got marshland on the right and house protected by a couple of trees on the left. My dad loves to swing for the fences, but on this hole, the high-risk play usually leads to a high score. To play this right, you have to manage the math. You take a club that clears the water comfortably but stops well short of the narrow trouble. You play for the "fat" part of the fairway and live to fight another day.

In the world of leadership, Dad explains that Hole 5 happens every week in the school administrative office. Every leader eventually faces a "Water Hazard"; a high-stakes project, a controversial new policy, or a redistricting plan that requires a "forced carry." Risk management in this context isn't about avoiding the water entirely; it's about knowing your team's "carry distance." You can't commit to a 200-yard carry if your staff only has 170 yards of "swing" in them. If you overpromise and land in the marsh, morale sinks instantly. Furthermore, you have to identify the "woods." Sometimes a win at all costs leads to a sand trap of human resource (HR) issues or a forest of community backlash. Sometimes, the most leader-like thing you can do is lay-up. It is better to take a safe, calculated approach that guarantees you're in a position to score on the next shot than to go for the hero play and end up disqualified.

Ultimately, risk management is the art of choosing the smart shot over the spectacular one. It's about ensuring that even your misses leave you in a position to recover rather than out of the tournament. As we wrap up this hole, I want you to reflect: are you currently swinging for the fences on a project where a calculated lay-up would actually guarantee a better long-term result? Remember, the scorecard doesn't have a column for how far you hit it, only for how many strokes it took. Check your ego at the tee box, take more club (the next size club that carries more distance) than you think you need to clear the hazard, and keep your eye on the long game.

We both landed our drives safely in the fairway and both hit our approach shot on the green. All that's left is to send the ball home.

Mission accomplished! Two pars!

Hole #5 Score Card: Risk Management

1 - I have mastered this skill

2 - I'm pretty good in this area

3 - I want to be better in this area

4 - I really struggle in this area

5 - I have no idea why this is important

Hole #5 Date (M/D/Y)	**Golf Score** Avoiding Hazards: Choosing the smart shot over the spectacular shot	**Leadership Score** Risk Management
__/__/__		
__/__/__		
__/__/__		
__/__/__		

Hole # 6: Reading The Wind

Hop in your golf cart. I (Dad) am going to do the talking this hole.

I grip the steering wheel of the cart like it's a lifeline, steering us away from the green of Hole 5. We just finished talking about risk management and how to weigh the odds before pulling a club out of the bag. But as we bump along the path toward the 6th hole at the Woodlands Golf Course in Hampton, Virginia, I can feel the wind start to whip off the Chesapeake Bay, shaking the frame of the cart.

"Listen, Ivy," I say over the rattle of the clubs. "Risk management is great in theory, but it's useless without "Situational Awareness." You can have a perfect plan for a 150-yard shot, but if you aren't aware that the ground is soggy from last night's rain or that the wind is gusting at 20 mph, your plan is just a fast track to a double bogey. In leadership, if you don't keep your head on a swivel to see the external shifts in your district or your building, you're flying blind."

That reminds me, I have to tell you about a time my internal "Situational Awareness" saved my life, or at least my college career.

It was my sophomore year in college and a few of my boys and I were itching to get out of town for the weekend. We heard about a massive party down in North Carolina, but there was one problem: none of us had a reliable ride that could make the trip.

Here comes a "new guy" someone had just met a few weeks prior. He was flashy, high-energy, and most importantly, he had a car and was offering to drive the whole crew to North Carolina. On paper, the plan was a "Birdie." We had the destination, the crew, and the transportation.

But as we were standing in the parking lot, throwing our bags in the back, the "wind" shifted.

I looked at the driver. He was too eager, too rushed. I looked at the car, no personal items, no trash, and a license plate that was in the back seat. My gut started screaming. It wasn't a logical "math" problem I could solve; it was a physical feeling in my chest that said, *something is off with this environment.*

At the absolute last second, I pulled my bag out of the trunk. "Go ahead without me," I told them. "I need to stay back and study for my test on Monday."

My friends roasted me. They called me "Old Man Byrd" and "scared." They laughed as they pulled out of the lot, heading for the highway.

The next day I got the call. They never made it to the party. They were pulled over just across the North Carolina border. It turns out my "gut feeling" was right. The driver hadn't just "borrowed" that car; it was reported stolen two days prior. Everyone in that car was handcuffed and taken down to the police station for questioning.

The Lesson: In leadership, you can have a perfect plan and a willing team, but if your "internal radar" tells you the person leading the charge or the vehicle you're using is compromised, listen to it. Situational awareness isn't just about looking at the trees to see the wind; it's about sensing the vibration of the room.

If the "vibes" are off, don't get in the car.

Reading the Wind (Ivy's Take)

We finally pull up to Hole 6 at The Woodlands. After shaking off the horror of that story that could have changed my dad's life, I lock back in to the task at hand. Hole 6 is a test of character. It's a relatively straight Par 5, but it's framed by trees and more. This is a great course for beginners because it's pretty easy to find your ball if you miss left or right. However, on this day, the openness of the course leaves it completely exposed to the elements. Today, the wind isn't just a breeze; it's a "howler." It's blowing hard from right to left and directly into our faces.

Dad grabs his driver and starts his usual routine, but I stop him.

"Dad, you just finished lecturing me about situational awareness. Look at the tops of those pines. Look at the ripples on the water hazard to the left. If you try to hit your normal high-arching 'moon ball' drive, that wind is going to catch it like a kite and dump it in the drink."

To play this hole well today, we aren't playing the course; we're playing the elements. We need to keep the ball low, "stinger" style, to stay under the gust. We have to aim further right than feels comfortable to account for the drift.

The Golf Lesson: Adjusting for the Elements

In golf, the "perfect swing" doesn't exist in a vacuum. You have to account for the External Variables:

The Wind: It dictates your club choice (take two extra clubs when hitting into it).

The Turf: Is it firm or soft? That changes how much the ball will roll.

The Pressure: Are you up by two or down by ten?

If you play the yardage on the marker without looking at the environment around you, you're letting the course win.

The Leadership Lesson (Dad's Take)

Ivy is right, the wind changed the game before we even took a swing. In leadership, we call this the "External Environment."

You might have a brilliant "Strategic Plan" (your yardage marker) for the school year. But then, an external "wind" hits: a change in state legislation, a sudden budget cut, or a shift in community sentiment.

Situational Awareness means you stop looking at your notes and start looking out the window.

Read the Room: Just like checking the grass to see which way the wind is blowing; a leader must sense the morale of the staff before dropping a new initiative.

Adjust the Trajectory: If the political or social climate is "windy," you might need to keep your goals "lower to the ground"; focusing on small, certain wins rather than high-lofted, risky projects that could get blown off course.

Don't Fight the Force: You can't out-yell the wind. You have to work with it. If the community is demanding a certain change, align your "aim" to account for that pressure.

Closure: Putting it Together

Great golfers and great leaders share one trait: they are never surprised by the weather. They observe, they adjust, and they execute based on the *current* reality, not the *ideal* conditions. Ivy's low stinger and my adjusted aim showed that you can't change the wind, but you can certainly change your stance. Great leaders don't complain about the climate; they adjust their sails, and their swings, to master it. We write down our pars on the score card and slide in the golf cart.

Reflection Question

What is the "howling wind" currently affecting your organization, and are you still trying to hit a "high-arc" shot despite it?

____

____

Related Golf Tip: *"When it's breezy, swing easy."* Don't try to overpower the wind. Taking more club and swinging at 75% power keeps the ball lower and more controlled.

Hole #6 Score Card: Situational Awareness

1 - I have mastered this skill
2 - I'm pretty good in this area
3 - I want to be better in this area
4 - I really struggle in this area
5 - I have no idea why this is important

Hole #6 Date (M/D/Y)	**Golf Score** Ability to read the wind	**Leadership Score** Situational Awareness
__/__/__		
__/__/__		
__/__/__		
__/__/__		

Hole # 7: The Fine Print

"Man, Dad, watch the curb!"

I gripped the side of the golf cart as my dad took a sharp turn toward the 7th tee box at Sleepy Hole Golf Course. He was in a zone, talking a mile a minute about his "vision" for the back nine. He was so focused on the big picture; the final score, that he almost sent us into a drainage ditch.

That's my dad: high energy, big goals, and sometimes, a complete disregard for the obstacles right in front of his tires.

We stepped out onto the grass. Hole 7 is a beautiful, treacherous little Par 3. From the tee box, it looks simple. It's a straight shot. But if you look closer, and I mean really look, you'll see the trap.

The green is shaped like a kidney bean, guarded by a massive, hungry bunker on the front right. The wind was whipping off the Nansemond River, coming in from the left.

"I'm going right at it," Dad said, pulling his 7-iron.

"Dad, wait," I said, squinting at the green. "Look at the flag."

"I see it, Ivy. It's yellow. Let's go."

"No, look at the base of the flag. It's tucked three feet behind that ridge on the right. If you're short by an inch, that ball is rolling all the way back into the sand."

He didn't listen. He was too eager to make a move. He took a huge, aggressive swing. The contact sounded pure; a loud thwack that echoed off the trees. The ball soared, tracking perfectly toward the hole.

"That's a birdie!" he shouted, starting to walk before the ball even landed.

But then, the details took over. The wind caught the ball just enough to nudge it two feet to the right. It hit the very top edge of the ridge, paused for a dramatic second, and then, obeying the laws of gravity and green-side architecture, trickled backward, picking up speed until it disappeared into the soft, white sand of the bunker.

In golf, amateurs play "areas," but pros play "inches." My dad saw a green; I saw a topographical map. He saw a destination; I saw the hazards guarding the entrance. When you ignore the fine print of a golf hole: the wind speed, the slope of the fringe, the exact placement of the pin, you end up working twice as hard to fix a mistake that shouldn't have happened. You can have the best swing in the world, but if your aim is off by one degree, you're playing from the beach.

The Leadership Lesson: The Letterhead Lesson (Dad's Take)

Ivy is right. I learned that lesson the hard way long before I ever picked up a golf club.

When I was a brand-new Assistant Principal, I was hungry. I wanted my principal to know that I wasn't just a "placeholder"; I was a go-getter. I wanted to be the person who made her life easier.

We had a major community initiative coming up, and I volunteered to handle the communication. I spent hours crafting a letter to the parents. I polished the language. I made it sound professional and inspiring. Then, I went into "beast mode." I printed 900 copies. I hand-peeled 900 address labels. I stuffed 900 envelopes. The table in the conference room looked like a mail sorting facility.

The next morning, I marched into the principal's office and placed the heavy crates of mail on her desk. I was beaming. I was waiting for the "Good job, Stenette, you're a rockstar."

She smiled, picked up one envelope, pulled out the letter, and read it. Her smile faded.

"Stenette," she said. "This is a great letter. But look at the second paragraph."

I looked. Right there, in the middle of a sentence about 'educational excellence,' was a typo. I'd written 'their' instead of 'there.'

"It's just one letter, right?" I whispered, my heart sinking. "I doubt anyone will even notice."

She looked me dead in the eye. "This letterhead has my name at the top as Principal. If we send out 900 letters with a mistake, we are telling 900 families that we don't value accuracy. We are telling them we are sloppy. If we can't get a letter right, why should they trust us to get their child's education right? Recycle these. All of them. And do it again."

I spent the rest of the day redoing my work. I realized then that speed is never an excuse for sloppiness. Leadership isn't just about the "big vision;" it's about the integrity of the details.

Precision is a form of respect. When you pay attention to the details, you show your team and your "customers" that the work matters. Whether it's a 150-yard shot or a 1-page memo, the small stuff is what keeps you out of the sand.

Ivy's par was won in the details, while my double-bogey was lost in the "fine print" of the green's ridge. In any organization, the small details you overlook today will become the steep hills you have to climb tomorrow.

Reflection Question: *Where are you moving so fast that you might be missing a "typo" in your leadership?*

____

____

____

Related Golf Tip: Check your alignment on every single shot. Most "bad swings" are actually just "bad aim." Lay a club down at your feet on the range to make sure your body is actually pointing where your brain thinks it is.

Hole #7 Score Card: Attention to Detail

1 - I have mastered this skill
2 - I'm pretty good in this area
3 - I want to be better in this area
4 - I really struggle in this area
5 - I have no idea why this is important

Hole #7 Date (M/D/Y)	**Golf Score** Willingness to adjust based on the undulations of the green and placement of the pin	**Leadership Score** Showing Attention to Detail
__/__/__		
__/__/__		
__/__/__		
__/__/__		

Hole # 8: Trampolines And Territory

We're off to the 8th tee box at Riverfront. As we pull up, we take a long look down the fairway. This isn't just a hole; it's a journey. It is a massive, Par 5 that seems to stretch out toward the horizon until the green is nothing more than a tiny white speck. When you stand here, you don't think about the pin; you think about survival. The 8th hole is designed to test your resolve. To your left, a row of houses protected by trees, and to your right, a thick tree line that waits to swallow any ball that isn't struck with absolute focus. It is the kind of hole that makes an amateur want to swing out of their shoes just to get the agony over with.

As we step onto the grass, Dad grabs his driver with a look in his eye that tells me he wants to kill the ball again. I have to step in and settle him down. I tell him, "O.G., you can't win this hole on the first swing. You just need to find the short grass." He manages a decent drive, but as we roll up to his ball, we realize we still have over 300 yards to go. The wind starts picking up, blowing right into our faces. We hit our second shots, and we're *still* not there. It feels like we've been on this one hole for an hour. This is the "grind"; the part of golf that requires pure patience and physical endurance.

The Golf Lesson: Don't Chase the Hero Shot

The biggest mistake you can make on a long Par 5 is trying to make up for the distance all at once. When golfers get tired or frustrated by the length of a hole, they start chasing the "hero shot." They try to hit a 3-wood out of a thick lie or aim for a tiny window between trees just to save a stroke. In reality, success on a long hole isn't about one spectacular hit; it's about a string of smart, disciplined decisions. You have to endure the distance and stay patient enough to wait for your real opportunity to attack the pin. If you lose your cool on shot two, you'll never even see the birdie putt on shot four. You have to play the hole as it is, not as you wish it were.

The "Trampoline" Strategy

My dad listens to my golf advice, but I can see his mind turning toward a different kind of endurance. This hole reminds him of the early days of the COVID-19 pandemic. Talk about a long Par 5; as leaders, we couldn't see the green, and we certainly didn't know where the hazards were hidden. During that time, my sister, our next-door neighbors, and I had exactly one outlet; the backyard trampoline. It was our sanctuary. It kept us active, kept us sane, and kept us out of trouble while the rest of the world felt like it was falling apart. Then, the letter came. The Homeowners Association (HOA) demanded we remove it because it could be seen from the street.

Dad was livid. In the middle of a global crisis, the bureaucracy was worried about a view from the curb. His first instinct was to fire off a scorched-earth email; the leadership equivalent of swinging out of his shoes and ending up in the marsh. Instead, he decided to play the long game. He sat down and wrote a letter that was a masterclass in standing your ground with logic and grace. He explained that the trampoline wasn't an eyesore; it was a mental health tool. It provided a safe, socially distanced space for children to exercise and find joy during a time of unprecedented isolation.

He didn't just ask for permission; he set a firm boundary. He told the HOA that he would not be removing the trampoline until the pandemic was over. He gave them two clear options: they could continue to waste resources sending letters, which he informed them he would promptly ignore, or they could realize that a global pandemic required a level of grace and understanding that was more important than the neighborhood aesthetic codes. He chose the endurance of a well-reasoned argument over the "hero shot" of an angry outburst. He knew that by protecting his children's "safe space," he was winning the long game of parenting and leadership, even if the HOA didn't like the view from the street.

As the pandemic restrictions began to lift, we realized that while the trampoline had served its purpose as our "safe haven," its season in our yard had come to an end. True to our word, we decided to pay the blessing forward. We disassembled the frame and moved it to a neighbor's house. A family with young, high-energy kids and, most importantly, a sturdy, fenced-in backyard.

The most remarkable part of the story wasn't the move, though. It was the silence. From the moment the kids started jumping, I never received another letter. No more complaints, no more "territory" disputes, and no more anonymous notes. By protecting that small space for joy during a crisis, we didn't just survive the pandemic; we eventually outlasted the conflict

The 8th hole at Riverfront isn't won by the strongest golfer, but by the one who stays the course. Endurance isn't just about moving forward; it's about maintaining your integrity and your "why" when the finish line is nowhere in sight. When you face an unfair obstacle or a long stretch of professional fatigue, do you react with a "hero shot" fueled by impulse, or do you have the endurance to play the long game? Remember: on long holes, tension is the enemy. If your grip is too tight, your swing will fail before you reach the green.

I enter Dad's bogey and my par on the school card. I maintained my pace while Dad resisted the urge to rush the long walk.

Reflection Question

When you are in the middle of a "long walk," whether it's a 550-yard hole or a year-long organizational crisis, are you making decisions based on the frustration of the moment, or are you protecting the 'safe spaces' and core values that will get you to the finish line?

Identify your 'Trampoline." What is the one thing in your organization or family right now that is keeping morale high, but is being threatened by a rule, a critic, or a 'view from the street'?

Once you've named it, what is the logical, firm 'Letter' you need to write to protect that space until the crisis passes?

Hole #8 Score Card: Patience & Endurance

1 - I have mastered this skill

2 - I'm pretty good in this area

3 - I want to be better in this area

4 - I really struggle in this area

5 - I have no idea why this is important

Hole #8 Date (M/D/Y)	**Golf Score** Avoids trying to cover too much ground in one shot, on Par 5's	**Leadership Score** Showing Patience & Endurance
__/__/__		
__/__/__		
__/__/__		
__/__/__		

Hole # 9: The Mentor And The Mentee

I enter Dad's bogey and my par on the score card. We're almost halfway through the course when we pull the cart up to the 9th tee box at Bide-A-Wee Golf Course in Portsmouth. It's that point in the morning where the sun is starting to bake the fairway and the "front nine fatigue" begins to set in. The 9th is a critical juncture; it's the bridge between a strong start and a total collapse.

The 9th hole at Bide-A-Wee is a demanding Par 4. It's a hole that looks simpler than it is, which is exactly how it lures you into a trap. To the right, thick Virginia trees stand like a wall, ready to kill any slice. To the left, there's enough trouble to turn a birdie look into a double-bogey disaster. The green is elevated and guarded by sand, requiring you to know exactly how far you hit your clubs. There is no room for guessing here.

Dad and I both let it rip off the tee. I'm sitting pretty in the center of the fairway, but Dad has found the light rough on the right. As I walk over to help him find his line, I catch him doing something that every golfer, and every struggling leader, is guilty of. He has his phone out.

He's scrolling through a 30-second TikTok from a "swing guru" in a garage somewhere, promising that if he just "flattens his wrist" at the top, he'll hit it like Tiger. I can practically see the smoke coming out of his ears as he tries to reconcile that video with what his actual coach (me) told him last Tuesday and what some guy at the clubhouse told him over a burger.

"Dad," I say, reaching for his phone. "Put the 'Algorithm' away. You're listening to three different gurus and a dozen strangers who have never seen you swing a club. You're ignoring the one coach who actually knows your game."

In the age of social media, there is a "pro" on every scroll promising a magic fix. If you watch ten different videos, you'll end up with ten different swing thoughts. By the time you address the ball, your brain is a knotted mess of "hinge the wrist," "keep the head down," and "clear the hips." You aren't playing golf anymore; you're performing a mechanical autopsy in the middle of a fairway.

The best golfers I know have one swing thought. Just one. They filter out the noise and trust a single, proven source. If you want real growth, you have to stop chasing every viral tip and stick to a mentor who understands your specific swing. To help you filter that noise, I've curated videos that actually work for me and help me to keep things simple. You can find them at:

https://www.youtube.com/@LLFATG/playlists

Also, feel free to enjoy our post, located on our YouTube page:

https://www.youtube.com/@LLFATG/post.

The Leadership Lesson: Legacy Through Others

Dad tucked the phone away and looked at me. "You're right, Ivy," he said, taking his 7-iron. "Leadership is the same way. Everyone has an opinion on how to run a school district or organization, but if you listen to everyone, you end up leading no one."

He explained that throughout his career, he's had to develop a "leadership filter." He learned early on that mentorship isn't just about receiving advice; it's about choosing the right voices to listen to, the ones who have actually been in the trenches and seen the data. But more importantly, he talked about our responsibility to be that voice for others.

Dad's ultimate vision for his career isn't a high salary or a big title. His "Eagle" is the ability to walk into a room of top-tier administrators and realize he helped put half of them there. He always jokes that his "retirement plan" is to work a part-time job for someone he once mentored. That's the dream; to build people so well that they eventually surpass you. You haven't truly led until you've poured into someone else's growth so deeply that they become the leader they once dreamed of being.

Success in golf and leadership depends on who you allow into your ear. Filter out the "social media" noise and focus on deep, intentional mentorship that builds a legacy.

Reflection Question: Are you currently listening to "experts" who don't know your heart, or are you leaning into a mentor who can help you reach your specific destination?

Related Golf Tip: The One-Thought Rule. Before you take your shot, identify one—and only one—thought (like "smooth tempo" or "finish high"). Once you have more than one thought, you've already lost the hole.

As we head to the clubhouse, my par and Dad's bogey highlighted the power of a single "swing thought." True mentorship isn't about adding complexity; it's about simplifying the game so everyone can finish strong.

Hole #9 Score Card: The Mentor and the Mentee

1 - I have mastered this skill

2 - I'm pretty good in this area

3 - I want to be better in this area

4 - I really struggle in this area

5 - I have no idea why this is important

Hole #9 Date (M/D/Y)	**Golf Score** Ability to focus on only one swing thought	**Leadership Score** Mentoring and Mentorship
__/__/__		
__/__/__		
__/__/__		
__/__/__		

The Turn

We've just finished the first nine holes, and we have reached what golfers call "The Turn." The Turn is more than just a place to grab a hot dog and a Gatorade at the clubhouse. It is a powerful moment for self-reflection and goal setting. On the golf course, the back nine offers a clean slate. It is the time to let go of the balls you lost in the woods on Hole 4 and the three-putts from Hole 7. It's about re-energizing yourself for the challenge ahead.

In leadership, we rarely give ourselves permission to take a "Turn." We carry our mistakes from one quarter to the next until we are weighed down by them. Let's change that right now. Take a moment to look at your leadership scorecard from the front nine.

Use the scorecard on the next page to evaluate yourself in each of the identified leadership categories discussed in the first 9 chapters.

The Scorecard: The Front 9

1 - I have mastered this skill

2 - I'm pretty good in this area

3 - I want to be better in this area

4 - I really struggle in this area

5 - I have no idea why this is important

Hole	Chapter Title	The Leadership Attribute	Self-Assessment Score
1	The Tee Box	Vision And Setting The Tone	
2	The Trap Of The Big Stick	Discipline And Restraint	
3	The Hidden Graveyard	Strategic Agility	
4	Out of the Pit And Into The Sand	Resilience And Grit	
5	The High Stakes Of The Hazzard	Risk Management	
6	Reading The Wind	Situational Awareness	
7	The Fine Print	Attention To Detail	
8	Trampolines And Territory	Patience And Endurance	
9	The Mentor And The Mentee	Mentoring And Mentorship	
		Total Score (Front 9)	

After reflecting on your score, take a moment to write down 3 personal goals for yourself in your leadership journey.

Goal # 1:

____

____

____

____

____

____

Goal # 2:

____

____

____

____

____

____

Goal # 3:

____

____

____

____

Hole # 10: Seizing Opportunities

We've just made the turn. We grabbed a couple of Gatorades and a snack at the clubhouse, and now we're staring down the back nine. I told Dad to let me take the lead on this one. Usually, he's the one dropping knowledge while I'm trying to keep his head down, but I had a story from my time in Kappa League, a youth leadership program led by the men of Kappa Alpha Psi Fraternity, Inc. I was serving as the Kappa League chapter President at the time, and the lesson I learned during one particular workshop has stuck with me longer than any leadership tip he's ever given me.

We were sitting in a massive, echoing auditorium with hundreds of other young men. The guest speaker stood at the podium, reached into his pocket, and pulled out a crisp bill. He held it high in the air for everyone to see. He didn't give a long-winded speech or a complex set of instructions. He simply said, "Who wants this money?" The room went crazy. Everyone was yelling "I do!" with their hands raised high. My peers were trying their best to get his attention. I didn't let myself overthink it; I calmly stood up and started walking toward the stage. It wasn't until I was halfway down the aisle that the rest of the room snapped out of it. Suddenly, chairs were slamming and guys were sprinting to beat me to the front. But I had the jump. By the time they reached the stairs, the money was already in my hand. I learned that day that while others are busy talking, yelling or doing nothing, the person who acts with courage is the one who secures the prize.

Dad looked at the 10th hole at Bide-A-Wee, then back at me. It's a classic dogleg left. From the tee box, you can't even see the green because a thick wall of trees guards the corner, and the fairway looks like it disappears into the forest. Because this is a Par 5, most golfers play it safe, hitting a mid-iron to the center of the fairway just to see the target. But for those with the distance, there's an opportunity to cut the corner and leave a tiny chip shot for birdie. This time it was Dad who noted that in golf, a dogleg is a test of "Calculated Aggression." Most golfers stand on a tee box like this and hesitate. They see the hazard instead of the opportunity on the other side. Because they are afraid of the "what ifs," they play it too safe and end up making the hole much harder than it needs to be. To "get the money" on a dogleg, you have to commit to the line. Hesitation mid-swing is what causes the ball to slice into the woods.

As a leader, you will often find yourself in these "auditorium moments." A new grant becomes available, a high-level position opens up, or a crisis requires someone to step up and lead a committee. Many people, even very talented ones, will sit in their seats and wait for a formal invitation or a clearer set of instructions. They are waiting for the perfect conditions. But fortune favors the bold, and it specifically rewards the first mover. In your organization, don't wait for the "all clear" signal to innovate. If you see a way to improve your culture or a gap that needs filling, move toward the stage. By the time your competition or your critics realize what's happening, you'll already be holding the results.

Success often goes to the person willing to look a little "confusing" to others by moving while everyone else is still sitting down. Whether it's cutting the corner on a dogleg or claiming a leadership opportunity, speed and courage are your best clubs. Ask yourself: What is the "money on the stage" in your professional life right now that you've been hesitant to go and grab? When playing a dogleg, pick a specific target *above* the tree line to keep your eyes up and your swing through the ball. Don't just watch the opportunity, take the jump.

Dad's Closing Thoughts

As we head toward the next hole to close out this chapter, I have to share a story about the moment I learned what "seizing opportunities" actually looks like. Early in my career, while finishing my Master's at Old Dominion University, I was given the chance to serve as a summer school administrator intern for Hampton City Schools.

My mentor at the time handed me the keys, stepped back, and essentially let me run the entire program with almost no direction. Now, I've worked with plenty of aspiring leaders who would have spent that summer complaining. They would have cried about a lack of support or used their mentor's hands-off approach as a pre-built excuse for anything that went sideways.

But I saw it differently. I realized early on that I was on my own, so I grabbed the wheel. I took total ownership, treated the program as my own, and learned through the fire.

Fast forward just a few months; I was sitting in an interview for an Assistant Principal position at the age of twenty-four. Because I had seized that summer opportunity instead of complaining about it, I didn't have to talk about "theories" or "potential." I was able to look that committee in the eye and speak fluently about my real-world successes, my failures, and the direct impact I had already made. I truly believe that refusing to play the victim and choosing to seize that wide-open opportunity was the only reason I broke into administration at such a young age.

Starting the back nine with matching pars, we realized that the "turn" is the perfect time for a fresh start. When opportunity knocks on the tenth hole of your career, don't just open the door; swing for the green.

Hole #10 Score Card: Seizing Opportunities

1 - I have mastered this skill
2 - I'm pretty good in this area
3 - I want to be better in this area
4 - I really struggle in this area
5 - I have no idea why this is important

Hole #10 Date (M/D/Y)	**Golf Score** Taking the risky shot to position yourself for an easy layup on the next.	**Leadership Score** Seizing Opportunities
__/__/__		
__/__/__		
__/__/__		
__/__/__		

Hole # 11: The Sidehill Lie

Hole 11 at Bide-A-Wee is a long Par 4 that demands focus. But the real challenge isn't just the distance; it's the undulation. You can hit a decent drive right down the middle, but because of the way the land sits, you'll likely find your ball resting on an uneven lie.

As predicted, after our tee shot, we found our ball sitting on a slope where the grass was higher than our feet. In golf, when the ball is above your feet, the hill wants to pull your swing off-balance. If you swing like you're on flat ground, you're going to hook that ball straight into the tree line. You have to widen your stance, choke down on the club, and fight for stability.

The Unexpected Pivot

I was standing there, looking at my ball on that awkward slope, thinking about my first semester at Norfolk State University (NSU). At the time of writing this book, I'm in the DNIMAS program (Dozoretz National Institute for Mathematics and Applied Sciences), which is basically the "Special Forces" for math and science majors. It's a high-pressure, full-scholarship program that requires total balance.

At a recent meeting, I was prepared to play a supporting role. I stood up and nominated my friend for the position of Chaplain. I was comfortable. I was "on flat ground."

Then, the ground shifted. Someone nominated me for the same position. Suddenly, I was standing on a sidehill lie I hadn't prepared for. I didn't want the job. I didn't want the responsibility. Most of all, I had never even said a prayer out loud in my life. I was totally off-balance.

The Golf Lesson: Adjusting for the Slope

When you find yourself on an uneven lie, you can't use your "standard" swing.

- Find Your Center: You have to dig your cleats in deeper to find stability.
- Choke Down: Since the ball is closer to you (or further away), you have to adjust your grip.
- Accept the Curve: A sidehill lie will naturally make the ball curve. Don't fight it—aim for it.

I remembered what Dad always told his mentees: "Never close a door without looking inside." Even if the "lie" of the situation is uncomfortable, you stay in the stance, take the swing, and see where it lands. I accepted the nomination, hoping I'd lose. I won.

Dad's Leadership Lesson: Stability in the Uncomfortable

Ivy found himself in a "leadership sidehill lie." He was prepared to lead from the sidelines, but the "course" had other plans. In any organization, you will be hit with unexpected nominations, "voluntold" assignments, or crises that force you out of your comfort zone.

The "Open Door" Mentality: Leaders often miss their best opportunities because they are afraid of the "slope." If a door opens, walk through it. You can always decide to leave later, but don't quit before you've seen the room.

Developing New Muscles: Ivy had never prayed out loud. He lacked that specific "stability." By accepting the role, he didn't just help the group; he developed a new skill of public speaking and spiritual leadership, that he now enjoys.

Stability is Internal: On a slope, the ground is crooked, but your spine must stay centered. When a new responsibility is thrust upon you, rely on your core values (your preparation) to keep you upright while you navigate the new terrain.

Sometimes the most rewarding parts of your "round" come from the shots you didn't want to take. Staying balanced on an uneven lie is what separates a varsity leader from a weekend hacker.

Reflection Question: What is a "door" in your life that you are trying to keep closed simply because the responsibility makes you feel off-balance?

____

____

____

____

Related Golf Tip: On a sidehill lie where the ball is above your feet, the ball will naturally move to the left (for righties). Aim slightly to the right of your target and let the slope do the work.

Since most driving ranges are perfectly flat, practicing for that 11th-hole slope can be tricky. You have to get creative to simulate that "off-balance" feeling while you're stuck on a flat rubber mat or grass tee.

Here are three ways to work on uneven lies at the range:

1. The "Book Drill" (Simulating Uphill/Downhill)

Take an old book (or thick notebook) to the driving range and place it under one of your feet.

For Uphill: Place the book under your **lead foot** (left foot for righties). This forces your weight back and tilts your shoulders, mimicking a climb.

For Downhill: Place it under your **trail foot**.

The Goal: Practice making a smooth 75% swing without falling over. If you can stay balanced with a book under your foot, a hill at Bide-A-Wee will feel easy.

2. Shift Your Weight Distribution (Simulating Sidehill)

You can't easily tilt the ground at the range, but you can simulate the effect of the slope on your body:

Ball Above Feet Simulation: Stand a little closer to the ball and put more weight on your **toes**. This mimics the feeling of being pushed backward by a slope. Focus on "choking down" on the grip and swinging more like a baseball bat (flatter plane).

Ball Below Feet Simulation: Stand slightly further away and sit back into your **heels**. This mimics the feeling of the ground falling away from you. Focus on keeping your knees bent deeply throughout the entire swing.

3. The "Staggered Stance" Drill

This is great for general stability.

Drop your trail foot back about 6 inches so only your toe is touching the ground.

Try to hit a 7-iron while balancing almost entirely on your lead leg.

This works because it forces you to find your "internal center." When you get to that uneven lie on Hole 11, your brain will already know how to keep your spine stable even when your feet aren't level.

Always remember the Rule of 75: On a slope, never swing at 100% power. Swing at 75% effort and use one extra club. The slope is already fighting your balance; don't give it more ammunition by trying to "kill" the ball.

Dad's Closing Message

As I managed to scramble my way onto the green from that awkward sidehill lie, I was so busy celebrating my "save" that I headed straight for the cart, puffing out my chest. But Ivy wasn't moving. He stood by the edge of the green, pointing back at the indentation my high-arching wedge shot had carved into the soft putting surface. "Not so fast, Pops," he said with a grin that was half-teacher, half-captain. "You can't just take the par and run. If everyone ignored their ball marks, this green would look like the surface of the moon by noon. You owe it to the players behind us to leave this place better than you found it." He tossed me my repair tool, reminding me that the quality of the course, and the integrity of the game, depends on every player taking responsibility for the impact they leave behind.

Ivy found stability, and a par, through technique, while I scrambled to a par by finding my balance on uneven ground. Leadership rarely happens on level turf, so learn to plant your feet firmly when the world starts to tilt.

Hole #11 Score Card: Balance & Stability

1 - I have mastered this skill

2 - I'm pretty good in this area

3 - I want to be better in this area

4 - I really struggle in this area

5 - I have no idea why this is important

Hole #11 Date (M/D/Y)	**Golf Score** Playing on an uneven surface	**Leadership Score** Balance and Stability
__/__/__		
__/__/__		
__/__/__		
__/__/__		

Hole # 12: Divots And Decisions

Ivy and I (Dad) pull up to the tee box of the 12th hole at Suffolk Golf Course in Suffolk. It's a beautiful, straight-ahead Par 4, playing about 340 yards from the white tees. On paper, it looks simple; other than the 70 yards of water, there are no major doglegs, no hidden tricks. But there is a deceptive row of trees on the left and a bunker guarding the front left of the green. It's the kind of hole that lulls you into a false sense of security. After a decent drive, I prepare for my approach shot. I take a deep breath, swing with everything I've got, and I catch it pure. The ball soars, landing dead center of the green. But as I begin to walk away, I see it: a deep, ugly trench where my club head delved too deep into the turf. I've reached the green in regulation, but I've left another wound in the turf behind me.

Leave it Better Than You Found It

In golf, a divot is an inevitability. If you're swinging correctly, you're going to take some turf. The rule of the game isn't that you must play perfectly; it's that you must be accountable for the impact you have on the course. To repair a divot, you either retrieve the sheared-off "toupee" of grass and fit it back into the hole like a puzzle piece, or you fill the void with a mixture of sand and seed. If you walk away without fixing it, the next golfer's ball might roll right into your crater, ruining their shot. Accountability on the course means realizing that your actions, even the successful ones, have a footprint. If you don't repair the damage, the course eventually breaks down for everyone.

The Leadership Lesson: Repairing the Trust Gap

In the world of education and organizational leadership, "taking a divot" is the equivalent of a lapse in judgment, a broken promise, or a communication breakdown. You might hit a "great shot" but if you ran over people's feelings or ignored the culture to get there, you've left a divot in the professional landscape. Accountability isn't just about admitting you hit a bad shot; it's about the "repair" work. When trust is broken, you can't just drive away and hope it heals. You have to go back to the person or the team, acknowledge the hole you left, and fill it with the "sand and seed" of transparency and genuine apology. Repairing trust is a manual labor job; you have to get your hands dirty to make things right.

Accountability is the glue that holds every organization's culture together. When a leader is willing to go back to the fairway and fix their mistakes, it gives the rest of the staff permission to be human too. It shows that you care more about the health of the "course" (the organization) than you do about your own convenience. If you want a team that takes ownership, you have to be the first one to step off the cart and fix the turf.

Reflection Question: Think about a recent decision you made. Did it leave a "divot" in your team's morale, and if so, have you gone back to fill it?

Ivy's Related Golf Tip: Always carry a sand bottle on your cart. It's much easier to fix a mistake when you have the right tools ready the moment the damage happens.

Ivy's clean approach and eventual par left no trace, but my bogey came with the integrity of a repaired divot. Every decision leaves a mark on your culture; make sure you're the kind of leader who leaves the course better than you found it.

Hole #12 Score Card: Accountability and Repairing Trust

1 - I have mastered this skill

2 - I'm pretty good in this area

3 - I want to be better in this area

4 - I really struggle in this area

5 - I have no idea why this is important

Hole #12 Date (M/D/Y)	**Golf Score** Repairing the ground, when necessary, after each shot	**Leadership Score** Accountability and Repairing Trust
__/__/__		
__/__/__		
__/__/__		
__/__/__		

Hole # 13: The High Stakes Of The Inner Circle

We're off again, in the cart, headed over to the 13th tee box at Sleepy Hole Golf Course. After the back-to-back challenges, and successes, of Holes 11 and 12, we're feeling the weight of the round. This is where the fatigue starts to set in, and where your focus on the "fundamentals" is either going to save you or sink you.

Hole 13 is a Par 5 that demands respect. It's not just about distance; it's about positioning. The marsh and the entrance road, lining the fairway, act like silent critics, waiting to snag any ball that isn't struck with confidence. If you try to do too much, you'll find yourself in big trouble.

We've just stepped off the tee. I hit a solid drive right down the center-cut. Dad? He's a bit off to the left, flirting with the tree line. As we walk toward his ball, he's already over-analyzing his next step (the swing plane, the grip pressure, and the wind speed). He's so focused on the mechanics of the shot that he's forgetting the most important factor: the executioner.

The Golf Lesson: Trust the Player, Not the Equipment

In golf, people love to buy the latest gadgets. They buy the "perfect" training program or the $600 driver because the marketing says it's a game-changer. But here's the reality: A great golfer can shoot par with a set of rusty garage-sale clubs, but a terrible golfer (sorry, Dad) will still slice a brand-new sleeve of balls into the woods, even with a brand-new set of Mizuno irons in his bag.

The "program" (the clubs, the swing theory, the yardage book) is secondary. The "person" (the golfer) is everything. If the golfer doesn't believe in the shot, or if their fundamentals are shaky, the most expensive equipment in the world won't save the scorecard. You have to invest in the player before you invest in the gear.

Dad's Leadership Lesson: People Before Programs

Ivy is right. In my years leading school districts, I've seen million-dollar "programs" fail miserably because the staff didn't believe in them. On the other hand, I've seen mediocre ideas succeed wildly because a group of dedicated, high-performing teachers grabbed an idea and ran with it.

Here is the hard truth for leaders: The disgruntled staff members usually speak the loudest. If you aren't careful, you'll spend 90% of your energy trying to appease the "squeaky wheels," the people who will complain no matter what you do.

When you yield to the loudest naysayers, you lose the trust of your top people. Your best performers are watching you. They want to see if you have the backbone to stand up for the organization's values. If your "A-players" support a move, do it! If the naysayers don't like it, they can get on board or find another course to play. Don't sacrifice your best people to satisfy your loudest critics.

A leader's most valuable committee isn't a formal board; it's the core group of high-performers who carry the culture. Programs don't drive results; people do. Stop managing for the bottom 10% and start leading for the top 10%.

Reflection Question

Who are the three "Top People" in my organization, and have I asked for their honest perspective on our current direction this week?

____

____

____

Related Golf Tip: Before you buy a new club to fix your hook, go see a pro for a lesson. It's usually the person holding the club, not the club itself, that needs the adjustment.

Hole #13 Score Card: The Inner Circle

1 - I have mastered this skill
2 - I'm pretty good in this area
3 - I want to be better in this area
4 - I really struggle in this area
5 - I have no idea why this is important

Hole #13 Date (M/D/Y)	**Golf Score** Avoids blaming or relying on the equipment	**Leadership Score** Building and maintaining a strong inner circle
__/__/__		
__/__/__		
__/__/__		
__/__/__		

Hole # 14: Finesse Over Force

After entering two bogeys on the score card, from hole 13, we head over to the 14th tee box at Riverfront Golf Club in Suffolk. By this point in the round, the Virginia humidity is usually sitting heavy on your shoulders. You look out from the tee and see a monster. This Par 5 is a long, winding beauty that hugs the marshes of the Nansemond River. To your right are a row of houses with massive glass windows and people hanging out in their pools, in their backyard.

My dad usually approaches this hole with what I call "The Superintendent Mindset." He sees 534 yards and thinks he can solve the distance with raw data and high-velocity impact. He grunts, swings hard enough to lose his hat, and since the wind is helping, he actually finds the short grass. We've navigated the fairway and the bunkers, and are now standing about 30 yards from the green.

Here is the problem: Riverfront is famous for its fast greens, and Hole 14 is no exception.

The green doesn't just sit there; it breathes. It slopes significantly toward the water, and because it's a Par 5, the groundskeepers love to tuck the pin in spots that feel borderline illegal. If you approach this with too much aggression, you aren't just missing the putt, you're watching your ball roll away from the hole. In other words, you can hit a perfect shot that ends up 40 feet away from the pin because you didn't account for the surface.

It's All About the Touch

My dad is standing there with his wedge, looking at the pin like it's a target he needs to hunt down. I have to grab his arm and remind him: "Dad, you don't hit a fast green; you feel it."

When the greens are this fast, your mechanics matter less than your touch. Touch is that internal calibration that tells you how much energy to transfer to the ball. On a slippery surface, aggression doesn't work. If you try to force the ball to the hole, the lack of friction on the green will punish you.

You have to play with finesse. You use a soft grip, and imagine you're holding a bird, not a hammer. You have to read the subtle "grease" on the grass. Sometimes, to get the ball to the hole, you actually have to aim ten feet to the right and let the slope do the work for you. You aren't the boss of the ball once it hits that surface; you're just a consultant. My dad listens to my advice and matches my par using finesse and foresight to aim in a direction different from his target.

The Leadership Lesson: Emotional Intelligence is Your "Touch"

Ivy is right. Earlier in my career, I walked into school buildings like I was hitting a driver, all power, all speed; trying to force results through sheer will. I thought leadership was about the power.

I remember a Tuesday afternoon that still makes me cringe. I was in a faculty meeting, laying out a new vision for student data. Out of nowhere, a veteran teacher made a snide comment, questioning my leadership and my connection to the classroom. It felt like a personal attack. My face got hot. My "Hampton grit" turned into "Hampton rage."

Instead of dealing with it in the moment, I sat in my office and stewed. I opened my laptop and fired off an angry email to the entire staff. I didn't just address her comment; I questioned the "commitment" of the whole building. I hit “Send” before I took a second breath.

I failed to account for the "slope" of the room. I had 99% of a staff that would go to war for me, but because of one person’s comment, I sent a "high-velocity" email that hit everyone. To my best teachers, that email felt like a slap in the face. I had "blown the ball" right off the green and into the water.

I learned two life-changing lessons about leadership "touch" that day:

The "Draft" Rule: It’s okay to be mad. Type out every fiery word you’re thinking—but **DON’T PRESS SEND!** Save it in your drafts. Go home. Sleep. Usually, the morning light shows you just how "fast" that green really was.

Sniper, Not Shotgun: If you have a problem with one person, address them directly. When you use a "shotgun" approach (mass email) for a "sniper" problem (one person), the person it’s intended for ignores it, and your best people get hurt.

On the 14th hole at Riverfront, a powerful drive gets you to the green, but only a surgeon’s touch keeps you there. Similarly, your degrees get you the job, but your Emotional Intelligence determines if people will actually follow you when things get slippery.

Reflection Question

Is there an email sitting in your "Sent" folder that you wish you could take back? What would have happened if you had waited 24 hours to "read the green"?

____

____

Ivy's Related Golf Tip: When you're standing over a high-pressure putt on a fast green, take three deep breaths. It lowers your heart rate and relaxes your hands, giving you the "surgeon's touch" instead of the "hammer's hit."

Hole #14 Score Card: Emotional Intelligence

1 - I have mastered this skill

2 - I'm pretty good in this area

3 - I want to be better in this area

4 - I really struggle in this area

5 - I have no idea why this is important

Hole #14 Date (M/D/Y)	**Golf Score** Demonstrating touch as you chip onto the green	**Leadership Score** Emotional Intelligence
__/__/__		
__/__/__		
__/__/__		
__/__/__		

Hole # 15: Playing It Where It Lies

It's Dad here. I'm going to do the talking on this hole. Off we go! The sun beats down on the fairways of Sleepy Hole Golf Course, and I'm standing over my ball in the tall fescue. What a terrible start to this fairly straight Par 4. About fifty yards ahead, my playing partners are casually leaning on their drivers in the center of the short grass. They've got custom-fitted clubs, swing speeds that would make a physicist weep, and handicaps in the single digits.

Then there's me. A math major from Norfolk State University (NSU) who knows exactly what the arc of my ball *should* look like, but instead, I've just calculated the trajectory of a "worm-burner" that barely cleared the ladies' tee.

In that moment, the temptation is to play *their* game. I want to pull out the 3-iron, swing out of my shoes, and try to miracle a shot onto the green just to prove I belong. But logic and the scorecards of a thousand bad rounds tells me otherwise. If I try to play their game with my swing, I'm going to end up carding a ten.

In leadership, we call this the "Comparison Trap." Forget the logic of the "Known Variables" As a leader, you often step into a new role and immediately start looking at the organization next door. You see their brand-new STEM labs, their veteran staff, or their shiny "Blue Ribbon" status. You start trying to implement their "swing" in your building.

But here is the mathematical truth: **Your leadership equation is dependent on your specific variables.** If I'm at NSU and I'm solving a complex differential equation, I can't just copy the answer from the guy next to me if he's working on a completely different problem set. In leadership, your "problem set" consists of *your* current budget, *your* specific teacher vacancy rate, and *your* community's unique culture.

Play Your Hand, Not Theirs

When I was growing up in Hampton, we didn't always have the newest gear, but we had a strategy. We knew how to move with what we had. In golf, "playing your hand" means acknowledging that while my buddy can carry the water hazard from 250 yards out, my logical move is to lay up, take the water out of the equation, and play for the bogey. My golf friends now refer to this logic as "Byrd Math."

A "bogey" in leadership isn't a failure; sometimes, it's a strategic win. It's the steady, 3% gain in literacy scores that stays consistent, rather than the flashy 10% jump that collapses the following year because it wasn't sustainable.

Practical Applications for the "Green" Leader

Audit Your Bag: Stop looking at the "clubs" (resources) the neighboring school has. List your own. Do you have a resilient PTA? A few "master" teachers who are anchors? That is your 7-iron. Learn to hit it pure every single time.

The "Local Knowledge" Strategy: At NSU, we talked about "The Yard." It was our territory. Your school is your territory. You know the "breaks in the green;" those subtle cultural nuances that an outsider wouldn't see. Use that local logic to make decisions that outsiders wouldn't understand but your people will respect.

Ignore the Gallery: In golf, people watch the long drive. In leadership, people cheer for the big, expensive announcements. But championships are won on the putting green—the quiet, repetitive, logical work of supporting teachers and keeping the buses running on time.

Play *your* hand. Trust *your* logic. Lead *your* organization.

I may be a "terrible" golfer compared to Ivy and my golf buddies, but I'm a successful golfer when I play against the course and stay true to my own math. When you step into that office tomorrow, don't worry about the "scratch golfer" superintendent in the next county. Play *your* hand.

Reflection Activity: The "Course Management" Audit

In mathematics, you can't solve for x+y if you're using the constants from a different equation. Use this worksheet to define your specific variables and stop playing the "other guy's" game.

Step 1: Identify the "Course Hazards"

List three challenges your organization is currently facing that you've been "wishing away" instead of planning around (e.g., *a 20% vacancy rate, an aging HVAC system, or low community trust*).

The Logic Check: If these are the "water hazards" on your course, stop trying to hit over them if you don't have the "swing" yet. How can you strategically "lay up" or navigate *around* these realities this year?

Step 2: Inventory Your "Bag"

Forget what the organization across town has. What are the three most reliable "clubs" in your specific bag right now (e.g., *A strong Mid-Atlantic culture of resilience, a dedicated front office staff, or a high-performing 3rd-grade team*)?

____

____

The Strategy: How can you lean on these strengths more heavily while you work on the "weaker clubs" in your leadership game?

____

____

Step 3: The "Comparison Trap" Deduction

The Target: Think of a leader or an organization you've been subconsciously trying to emulate.

The Mismatch: What "variable" do they have that you currently do *not* have (e.g., *A multi-million-dollar grant, a hand-picked staff, or 10 years of tenure*)?

The Pivot: Based on *your* current logic and *your* current staff, what is one initiative you can "drop" because it belongs to someone else's game?

____

____

Step 4: Define Your "Bogey"

In golf, "Par" is the expected score. For a 20-handicapper, a "Bogey" (one over par) is often a great result that keeps the round on track.

What does a "Leadership Bogey" look like for you this month? (Define a win that isn't flashy or perfect, but is logical, sustainable, and moves you closer to "breaking 90.")

Dr. Byrd's Final Thought: "The logic of the yard at NSU taught us that it's not about having the most; it's about doing the most with what you have. Don't let someone else's highlight reel dictate your game plan."

Ivy, with the birdie, accepted the course conditions, and I turned a bad lie into a strategic bogey. You can't always choose your circumstances, but you can always choose your response; play the ball where it sits and lead from there.

Hole #15 Score Card: Playing It Where It Lies

1 - I have mastered this skill
2 - I'm pretty good in this area
3 - I want to be better in this area
4 - I really struggle in this area
5 - I have no idea why this is important

Hole #15 Date (M/D/Y)	**Golf Score** Choosing the best path to a Bogey when a par is not likely	**Leadership Score** Leading *Your* Organization
__/__/__		
__/__/__		
__/__/__		
__/__/__		

Hole # 16: Leading Within The White Stakes

It's time for our next hole. Keep your eyes peeled; we're heading over to the 16th tee box at Bide-A-Wee. We are deep into the back nine now, and the Virginia humidity is starting to take its toll. This is usually the part of the round where my dad's "Old School" stamina starts to flicker, but on this hole, exhaustion isn't the primary enemy; it's always the ego. Hole 16 is a deceptive Par 4 that demands your full attention. As you stand on the tee box, you'll notice a row of thin, white stakes running tight down the entire left side. To the right, you've got scattered trees and thick rough that might ruin your afternoon, but the left side? That's "stroke and distance" territory. The fairway always looks narrower than it actually is because those white stakes represent a hard, unforgiving "Out of Bounds" line.

I watch as Dad steps up to the ball, chest out, feeling a bit too confident after a strategic bogey on hole 15. He decides he's going to "rip one" and try to cut the corner to leave himself a short wedge into the green. He completely ignores the boundary line, trying to flirt with the edge of the stakes to gain a tactical advantage. *Whack*. The ball starts off looking like a beauty, but then it develops a nasty little draw. It crosses that invisible line defined by the white stakes by maybe two inches. "That's playable, I can hit that back onto the grass!" Dad says, already reaching for his bag. I have to put my hand up. "Nope," I tell him. "White stakes, Dad. That's a penalty. You're hitting your third shot from right here on the tee."

In golf, the most dangerous lines aren't the ones you can see easily, like a massive water hazard or a deep sand trap; it's the out of bounds. You can play a heroic recovery shot out of a bunker, and you can take a lateral drop out of a pond, but once you cross those white stakes, you are off the map. This is a lesson in course management versus greed. Many golfers see a tight boundary and try to "cheat" it by aiming as close to the danger as possible to save distance. A smart golfer recognizes where the "No-Go" zone is and aims for the center of the fairway, even if it means a longer second shot. In this game, your integrity is your scorecard. If you move your ball an inch in the woods when no one is looking, or ignore an out of bounds stake because "it's basically on the line," you aren't playing golf anymore. You're just taking a walk in the grass.

From Dad's perspective, I'm the "rules police," but he's the first to admit that these white stakes are the only things that keep an organization from collapsing. He explains that in leadership, Ethics and Boundaries aren't just about avoiding the "big" crimes that make the evening news. It's about the small, quiet compromises in the "in-between" spaces. It's how you handle a confidential conversation about a staff member when you're tempted to vent, or how you allocate a budget when you think no one is auditing that specific line item. It's the "favors" you do for friends that flirt with official policy. When you are a leader, people are always watching your "aim." If they see you flirting with the boundary lines of ethics, they will feel entitled to cross them entirely. You have to set your internal stakes further back than the legal ones. If the policy says you can't do "X," a great leader doesn't try to do "X minus one." They stay in the middle of the fairway where there is no question of their integrity.

Dad finishes with a double bogey and I manage a par. As we turn toward the clubhouse, remember that whether you are on the 16th at Bide-A-Wee or in the front office of a school, the boundaries are there for a reason. Crossing them might seem like it saves you time or effort in the moment, but the penalty, a total loss of trust or a double-bogey on your reputation, is never worth the risk. Ask yourself: Where in your professional life are you "flirting with the white stakes," and what would happen to your team's culture if they followed your lead? On the course, if the trouble is on the left, tee your ball up on the left side of the box and aim toward the right-center. Use the geometry of the hole to protect your score, and use your values to protect your career.

Hole #16 Score Card: Ethics and Boundaries

1 - I have mastered this skill
2 - I'm pretty good in this area
3 - I want to be better in this area
4 - I really struggle in this area
5 - I have no idea why this is important

Hole #16 Date (M/D/Y)	**Golf Score** Considering Tee Placement and Aim from the Tee Box	**Leadership Score** Ethics and Boundaries
__/__/__		
__/__/__		
__/__/__		
__/__/__		

Hole # 17: The Five-Foot Foundation

It's now time to head to the 17th tee box at Heritage Oaks. We've spent this cart ride navigating the rolling hills of Harrisonburg, and honestly, Dad is holding it together better than usual. For me, this course feels like home; I played here back-to-back years for the Virginia Class 5 State Tournament in the fall of 2022 and 2023. I know where the wind hides and how the greens break. For Dad, this is all new. He's staring at his scorecard, realizing he's got a legitimate shot at breaking 90. The pressure is sitting right on his shoulders like a heavy golf bag.

The 17th at Heritage Oaks isn't just a short Par 3, it's a "gut-check" finish. It's roughly 130 yards of pure nerves. You're looking at a green protected by bunkers, and because it's the second to last hole, you usually have a gallery of people sitting on the clubhouse patio watching your every move. It's a stage, and Dad is definitely feeling the spotlight. We both hit great tee shots, one of those rare moments where the universe aligns. Both balls land soft and tracking, settling exactly five feet from the cup. As we walk up the hill toward the green, Dad is breathing heavily, partly from the walk, but mostly from the realization that a birdie here would be one step closer to his goal to break 90. He looks at me and says, "Man, this is a lot of pressure for a five-footer."

I looked at him and laughed because I knew he was already prepared for this. "Dad, you've already made this putt a thousand times," I reminded him. I thought back to our sessions at the Taylor Bend YMCA when he first introduced me to weightlifting. I wanted to stack plates and look strong immediately, but Dad was strict; I had to start with the light stuff, often just the bar. He insisted on control, forcing me to build the stabilizer muscles and get my movements synchronized before I was allowed to go heavy. Now, at 18, I'm seeing huge gains, but only because the foundation was set in that "boring" phase. It was the same with the putting drills I put him through. I reminded him of the "10-in-a-row" drill where I made him stand over a five-foot putt and sink ten straight. If he missed the ninth, he had to start over at one. He got frustrated and groaned, wanting to move on to the "fun" long putts. But because he did the monotonous work then, this five-foot putt under the clubhouse lights now feels like a piece of cake. High performance under pressure is just a byproduct of high discipline during practice. Dad took a breath, stepped up, and drained it. As we walked toward the 18th hole, he started breaking down the leadership side of that putt.

The Leadership Lesson (Dad's Take)

In school leadership, everyone wants the "Big Win;" the high-test scores or the major culture shift. But you don't lead an organization to a "Birdie" finish by focusing on the pressure of the deadline. You do it by focusing on the systems you built months ago. We call this building capacity. If a leader hasn't trained their staff on the "small" things, like how to analyze a single data point or how to handle one difficult conversation, they can't expect them to perform when the "State Evaluation" pressure is on. You build the small muscles of your organization during the quiet times so that when the stakes are high, the execution is automatic. If you've done the boring work of building a solid foundation, the high-pressure moments aren't scary; they are just another repetition.

Success isn't found in the moment of truth; it's revealed there. Whether it's a five-foot putt to break 90 or a final presentation to a board of directors, your performance is simply the sum of your preparation. Think about your own leadership: What "small muscle" or foundational system in your organization have you been neglecting because it feels too basic or boring?

____

____

To get your "putting" game in order, try the 10-in-a-Row drill: place a coin five feet from the hole and don't leave the green until you sink ten consecutive putts. Then try "Around the World," placing four balls at three, six, and nine feet around the cup. Clear the inner circle before you move back. These drills build the "must-make" confidence that turns a high-pressure moment into just another day at the office.

Hole #17 Score Card: Performance Under Pressure

1 - I have mastered this skill
2 - I'm pretty good in this area
3 - I want to be better in this area
4 - I really struggle in this area
5 - I have no idea why this is important

Hole #17 Date (M/D/Y)	**Golf Score** Demonstrating Confidence as You Putt From 5 Feet or Less	**Leadership Score** Performance Under Pressure
__/__/__		
__/__/__		
__/__/__		
__/__/__		

Hole # 18: Choosing The Right Team Members

It's finally time to head to the last hole, and there is no better place in Virginia to finish a round of golf than Hole 18 at Sleepy Hole Golf Course. This Par 4 is as beautiful as it is intimidating. As you look toward the horizon, your approach shot is to a green almost entirely surrounded by water. The view is spectacular, but the stakes are high. My dad and I both managed to find the short grass with our drives, leaving us in a prime position to finish strong. Dad is sitting at 140 yards out, and I'm sitting at 110 yards. We are close enough to see the flag, but that water hazard is a constant reminder that one bad choice or one wrong club could ruin the entire day.

The Crew You Carry

My dad always said that choosing the right team members is a lesson he learned the hard way, off the course. I've spent a lot of my life just wanting to be one of the guys, but I quickly realized that who you "ride" with determines your destination. There was a time when I just wanted to hang out and have a fun night with friends, but as the night progressed, they became intoxicated. Suddenly, I wasn't just a friend; I was the designated protector. I had no choice but to take the wheel and ensure everyone got home safely. It taught me that if you surround yourself with people who lack self-control, you spend all your energy managing their mistakes rather than pursuing your own goals. In golf, if you pick a club you don't trust to clear the water, you've already lost. In life, if your "team" creates hazards instead of helping you avoid them, you'll never reach the green.

The Protection of the Circle

My dad often tells a story that flips this perspective on its head. He was always fortunate to have a tight-knit group of friends, but there was one specific night when they wouldn't let him get in the car. At first, he was genuinely hurt; he felt "dissed" and excluded by the people he trusted the most. It wasn't until later that he learned the truth: they were protecting him from something illegal that was in that vehicle. His friend eventually told him, "Your future is too bright to be involved with what we had in that car." His friends weren't perfect, but they loved and protected him, and that is the definition of a true team member. They knew his value even when he was too caught up in the moment to see it himself.

Building the Organization (Dad's Take)

We have to connect this reality to the world of work and school. Whether you are a student leader, school leader or a CEO, the selection process is the most crucial step in your leadership journey. You cannot take this for granted as it is the foundation of everything you build. Your goal as a leader is to select the right people, provide them with the necessary support and guidance until they have developed their skills, and then (this is the hard part for most) get out of their way. A great leader doesn't micro-manage a professional team; they curate a group of "protectors" and high-performers who keep the organization out of the water.

The Final Putt

As we wrap up this 18th hole, remember that your success is a direct result of who you allow in your cart. A leader is only as effective as the team they build. If you select based on character and loyalty, your team will protect the organization's future even when you aren't looking. Take a long look at your roster today. Are they helping you to land your shot on the green, or are they the reason you're looking for a lost ball in the hazard?

Reflection Question: Are you selecting team members based on their current skills, or their ability to protect and elevate the mission of the organization?

Golf Tip: On a high-pressure approach shot over water, always take "more club" than you think you need. Most players end up in the water because they under-club and try to swing too hard. Trust your selection and let the club do the work.

Hole #18 Score Card: Choosing the Right Team Member

1 - I have mastered this skill
2 - I'm pretty good in this area
3 - I want to be better in this area
4 - I really struggle in this area
5 - I have no idea why this is important

Hole #18 Date (M/D/Y)	**Golf Score** Selecting the Club You Trust to Clear the Hazard	**Leadership Score** Choosing the Right Team Members
__/__/__		
__/__/__		
__/__/__		
__/__/__		

Ivy's approach shot lands in the sand, which for this hole, is not a bad outcome. His next shot out of the sand was brilliant, landing next to the hole for an easy par putt.

As for me (Dad), my finish was brutal. As mentioned earlier in this book, this final hole at Sleepy Hole Golf Course is beautiful but it is also surrounded by water. A terrible golfer, like me, knows exactly how to find the water. After a drop, a chip, and two putts, I continue to maintain my status of a "Terrible Golfer" trying to break 90.

In this final, "Bonus" chapter, Ivy and I want to leave you with two crucial closing thoughts that are fundamental to sustained success and well-being in any leadership role: prioritizing self-care and rediscovering the passion that fuels your purpose. It's easy in the relentless pace of leadership to neglect your own well-being, viewing self-care as a luxury rather than a necessity. However, just as a golfer needs rest and proper conditioning to perform at their best, a leader needs to recharge their mental, emotional, and physical batteries to lead effectively and avoid burnout. Equally important is reconnecting with *why* you embarked on this path in the first place. When the daily grind obscures the initial spark of passion, leadership can become a chore. Remembering the love for what you do, the impact you wish to make, the people you aspire to serve, reawakens your drive and resilience. Embrace these final reflections as you prepare for your next round, ensuring your leadership journey is not only impactful but also personally fulfilling.

Bonus Lessons From A Terrible Golfer

Finding Your Core: Swing Thoughts for Leaders

I (this is Dad speaking) hope you enjoyed this book born not on the PGA tour, but on the often-frustrating, yet always-enlightening, fairways of courses like Riverfront, Sleepy Hole and Bide-A-Wee, right here in the heart of Hampton Roads. As a proud graduate of Norfolk State University, a mathematics major who found his calling in educational leadership, and a self-confessed terrible golfer with a handicap that hovers stubbornly around 20, I've discovered that the journey from tee to green is remarkably similar to the path of leading a school. This book is a collection of relatable stories, often laced with the humbling realities of my golf game, all designed to offer practical, actionable wisdom for leaders who, like me, are striving for excellence even when the scorecard doesn't always show it. My inspiration? It's a beautiful blend of my incredible family, who consistently remind me of what truly matters; my long-suffering golf buddies, whose banter and unwavering friendship make every duffed shot a little more bearable; and my dedicated work family, the passionate educators and staff who inspire me daily with their commitment to our students.

Throughout these chapters, we've explored how the challenges and triumphs on the golf course provide a perfect metaphor for the complexities of leadership. You've heard tales from my upbringing in Hampton, Virginia, where resilience was a daily lesson, and how those roots shaped my perspective. We've laughed at my golf misadventures and then paused to consider the serious implications for your own leadership journey.

Enjoy What You Do or Find Another Profession/Hobby

One of the most recurring themes, whether I'm shanking a seven-iron or navigating a tough budget meeting, is the absolute necessity of joy. Golf, when it's good, is pure bliss. When it's bad, it can feel like a chore. The same holds true for leadership. If you're not finding genuine enjoyment in the work, the daily interactions, the problem-solving, the small victories, then it's time for an honest self-assessment. This isn't just about fleeting happiness; it's about a deep, abiding satisfaction that fuels your energy and passion. Just as I continue to chase that elusive perfect shot on the course, knowing that the pursuit itself brings me joy, leaders must cultivate and protect their professional satisfaction. If the well of joy runs dry, it might be time to find another profession or hobby that truly ignites your spirit. Your enthusiasm, or lack thereof, is contagious.

Be Kind to Yourself and Others Because Kindness Matters

On the golf course, it's easy to get frustrated with yourself. I've slammed clubs, muttered under my breath, and let a bad shot define my entire round. But I've learned that beating myself up only makes the next shot worse. The same applies to leadership: be kind to yourself. You will make mistakes. You will face setbacks. Imperfection is part of the human and leadership experience. Just as importantly, kindness matters immensely in how you treat your team, your students, and your community, just ask Dr. Garett Smith, former Superintendent in Staunton. A kind word, an empathetic ear, or a genuine thank you can shift the entire atmosphere of a school. Remember, the kindness you extend to others, especially when they falter, builds trust and creates a culture where people feel safe to take risks and grow.

Don't Do This Work Alone: Build a Team of Support

As a terrible golfer, I've learned I can't do it alone. I need my buddies to laugh with me, to offer a tip (even if I don't always take it), and to remind me that it's just a game. Leadership is no different. You cannot, and should not, do this work alone. Building a team of support (whether it's your administrative team, trusted colleagues, mentors, or even just a network of fellow leaders) is non-negotiable. These are the folks who will celebrate your victories and, more importantly, lift you up when you're in the rough. When the pressures of the job mount, when the stress becomes overwhelming, and when your mental well-being feels compromised, it is absolutely critical to reach out to your support team when you need help (Mental Health). Don't suffer in silence. They are there for you, ready to offer a listening ear, practical advice, or simply a reminder that you're not on this journey by yourself.

Finding Your True North: Spirituality and a Higher Power

Finally, throughout my life, from the pews of my childhood church in Hampton, to my current church in Suffolk (shout out to Pastor Steve), and to the quiet moments of reflection on the golf course, there has always been a deeper current of spirituality and a belief in a higher power. For me, this is the unwavering bedrock that sustains me through life's challenges, both on the golf course and in the demanding world of educational leadership. It's the source of inner peace when the external world is chaotic, the quiet confidence that even when things go awry, there's a purpose beyond my immediate understanding. This personal connection, this faith, provides an anchor, offering perspective, humility, and the strength to keep going, one swing and one leadership decision at a time. It reminds me that while I strive for excellence, ultimate control is beyond my grasp, and surrendering to that truth often brings the greatest freedom.

This book is a testament to the idea that lessons are everywhere, even in the most frustrating of hobbies. May your leadership journey be filled with resilience, joy, kindness, unwavering support, and the profound peace that comes from knowing you are part of something greater. Now, go forth and lead, knowing that even a terrible golfer can teach you a thing or two about getting the ball in the hole.

A Note on Artificial Intelligence in This Book

Now that we have explored the wild world where golf swings meet leadership lessons, we want to share a quick heads-up about something pretty cool that helped bring this book to life. As you might know, the landscape of Artificial Intelligence (AI) is evolving faster than a perfectly struck drive on a Par 5. At the time we were putting these thoughts down, there were very few regulations or clear requirements around how AI is used and referenced. But just like a good caddy can give you insights you might miss, AI played a small but significant role in shaping some of the elements you've read. Specifically, some of the clever titles for chapters and sections, and a handful of those smooth transition sentences that guide you from one idea to the next, got a little assistance from AI. Think of it as having a really smart brainstorming partner who occasionally offered up just the right turn of phrase.

Our stories, our experiences and our adventures (and misadventures) on the golf course, those are all 100% us. The leadership insights, the heart behind every lesson; that's all from the journey. AI just helped us polish a few edges and make the reading experience even more enjoyable for you. So, as you flip back through these pages, know that while the wisdom comes from the fairways and the classrooms, a little bit of future tech helped us deliver it to you in the most engaging way possible. Now, let's get back to practice!

The Future Of "The Terrible Golfer" Series

We aren't heading to the clubhouse just yet. We are taking a ride over to a place that is near and dear to our hearts: The First Tee Golf Course, which is part of the YMCA of South Hampton Roads.

If you like our leadership lessons, here is one more plot twist for you: At the time of writing this book, my dad serves as a member of the YMCA Corporate Board.

It is a huge honor. And honestly, it's where the philosophy of this book comes full circle.

First, we have to give a massive shout-out to the CEO of the YMCA of South Hampton Roads, Anthony Walters. Anthony understands that you don't build a community just by opening doors; you build it by opening minds.

He is leading the charge with First Tee, an international youth development organization that uses the game of golf to introduce inherent values to young people.

First Tee isn't just about teaching kids how to avoid a slice (something my dad is still working on). Through after-school and in-school programs, they are shaping the lives of young people from all walks of life by reinforcing values like integrity, respect, and perseverance.

And trust me, it's making a difference.

This isn't amateur hour. The staff and volunteers at First Tee Hampton Roads include PGA professional consultants and a team of qualified golf instructors who assist in all programs under professional supervision.

They are running a serious lineup of programs designed to get kids active and focused.

When we are out there, we aren't just looking at fairways; we are looking at the future. We are watching our youth learn that the respect required to repair a divot is the same respect required to lead a team later in life.

"First Tee – Hampton Roads," YMCA of South Hampton Roads, accessed February 1, 2026, https://www.ymcashr.org/locations/first-tee-hampton-roads.

Our Vision: Taking This Book on Tour

My dad and I realized something while writing this. The lessons we learned on our local course apply everywhere, but every golf course has its own unique story, its own signature holes, and its own community.

So, we have a plan. We want to support youth golf programs not just here in Virginia, but everywhere.

Here is the offer: We want to partner with your local golf course to create a custom "Course Edition" of this book.

We don't want this to just be a book on a shelf; we want it to be a tool for your junior golfers and a fundraiser for your mission.

How The Partnership Works:

We can tailor *Leadership Lessons From The Son Of A Terrible Golfer* to fit your specific home course.

Your 18 holes: We will replace our local chapters with a focus on your course's layout.

Full-Color Visuals (optional): The book can feature high-quality, full-color photos of your 18 holes.

Custom Strategy: We will break down the specific hazards and strategies for your course (I'll handle the golf tips; Dad will handle the leadership translation).

The "50/50" Promise:

This is the most important part. We aren't doing this for profit; we are doing this for the pipeline.

For every custom book sold at your course, 50% of the proceeds will be given directly back to support the youth golf program at that specific course.

The Curriculum:

Because this book is short, punchy, and visual, it works perfectly as a Youth Curriculum. Junior golf instructors can use the book to teach the "Hole of the Week."

On the Range: The kids learn the swing mechanics required for that hole.

In the Classroom: They read the "Leadership Lessons" to learn about focus, resilience, or integrity.

Final Thoughts:

My dad might hit the ball into the water, but his heart has always been on solid ground. We believe that if you can teach a kid to respect the course, you can teach them to respect themselves.

If you run a course, manage a First Tee program, or just want to see your local 18 holes turned into a leadership manual, reach out to us.

Let's fix some swings. Let's build some leaders. See you on the First Tee (pun intended).

Sample Lesson Plan: Week 1

Theme: Integrity & Recovery

"Play It As It Lies"

Target Audience: Ages 10–14 (Birdie/Eagle Level) Duration: 60 Minutes Location: Putting Green & Short Game Area

---

I. The Setup (5 Minutes)

Instructor: Local Pro or Stenette IV

The Hook: Ask the group: *"Who here has ever made a mistake on a test? Who here has ever hit a terrible golf shot?"*

The "Terrible Golfer" Context (Read Aloud):

"In Chapter 4, Dr. Byrd (the Terrible Golfer) hits his drive directly behind a massive oak tree. No one is watching. He could easily kick the ball out into the fairway and have a perfect shot. But he doesn't. He takes his medicine, chips out sideways, and makes a Bogey. He calls this 'The Integrity Tax.' If you cheat the course, you never actually learn how to recover."

II. The Golf Skill: The "Trouble Shot" (20 Minutes)

Instructor: Local Pro or Stenette IV

Concept: We are learning how to hit a "Punch Shot" or a low chip to get back into position safely, rather than trying a hero shot through a tiny gap.

The Drill: "Tree Trouble"

Place alignment sticks or pool noodles in the ground to simulate "trees" blocking the direct line to the hole.

Drop balls in "bad lies" (deep rough, divots, or behind the sticks).

The Goal: Students must chip the ball *around* or *under* the obstacle to a safe zone (a hula hoop placed on the green), NOT directly at the pin.

The Rule: If they hit the "tree" (stick), they must count a penalty stroke.

III. The Leadership Lesson: Owning It (15 Minutes)

Instructor: Mentor or Volunteer

Gather the students in a circle.

Discussion: In golf, you can't blame the wind or the club if you slice it into the woods. You have to walk into those woods, find your ball, and deal with it.

The "Dad" Principle:

Dr. Byrd says leadership is the same way. When you mess up a project at school or forget your chores at home, you can't lie about it. You have to 'Play it as it lies.' Admitting you were wrong is the 'punch shot' of leadership—it gets you back on the fairway so you can keep moving forward.

Discussion Questions:

Why is it harder to be honest when no one is watching?

How does it feel when you admit a mistake versus when you try to hide it?

Why do we trust leaders who admit when they are wrong?

IV. The Challenge: The "Honest Scorecard" Game (15 Minutes)

Activity: A putting contest with a twist.

Students pair up.

One student putts 3 holes; the other student watches but *cannot* speak.

The putter must announce their own score out loud after finishing.

If the putter announces the wrong score (accidentally or on purpose), the partner corrects them.

The Win: The team with the most accurate scorekeeping (not necessarily the lowest score) wins the "Integrity Award" for the day.

V. The Takeaway (5 Minutes)

Homework: This week, catch yourself making a small mistake (at home or school). Instead of hiding it, own it immediately. Tell your parents or teacher, "I messed that up, here is how I'm going to fix it."

Closing Chant: *"Bad shots happen. Leaders recover. Play it as it lies!"*

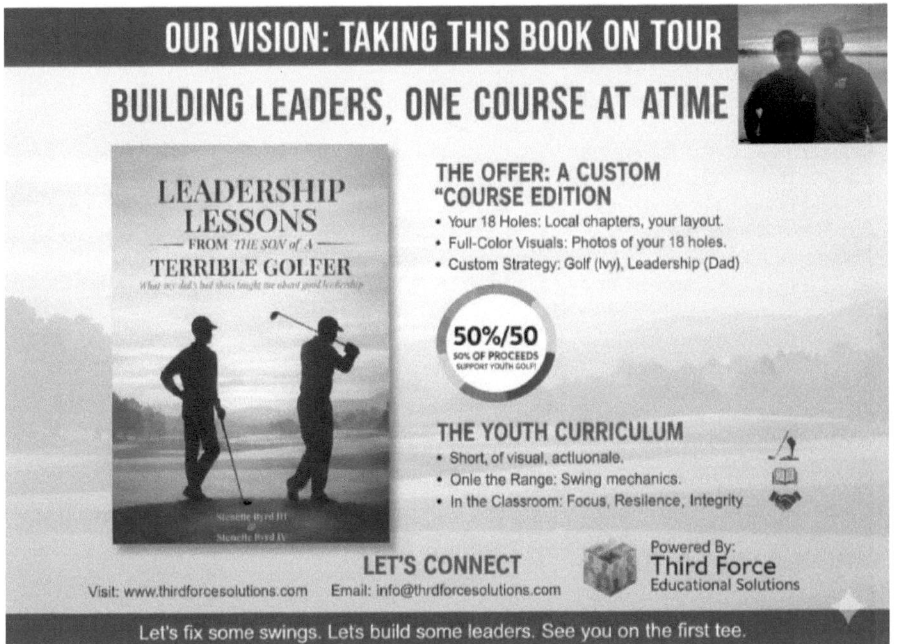

Learn More / Contact Us

www.thirdforcesolutions.com

About The Authors

Dr. Stenette Byrd III is a veteran educator and leader whose career began in 1997 teaching mathematics in Hampton, Virginia. By age 24, he stepped into administration as an assistant principal in Hampton City Schools, marking the start of a distinguished path that has led to his current role as Chief of Schools for Suffolk Public Schools.

Beyond his administrative leadership, Dr. Byrd is a prolific writer. He is the author of *Leadership Lessons from a Terrible Golfer* and co-author of *Leadership Lesson from the Son of a Terrible Golfer.* He has also co-authored influential educational texts such as *Stem Century: Suffolk Edition* and *Simple Solutions to Stubborn School Problems: A 70 in 7 Story.*

Dr. Byrd's leadership experience spans every level of K-12 education, having served as Principal for elementary, middle, and high schools across the region. He also shares his expertise in higher education as an adjunct professor at Old Dominion University and formerly at Norfolk State University.

A graduate of Norfolk State University (B.S.), Old Dominion University (M.Ed.), and The College of William and Mary (Ed.D.), Dr. Byrd balances his professional achievements with his devotion to his family. He is the proud parent of twins, Stenette IV and Trae Denise, and is a dedicated member of Kappa Alpha Psi Fraternity, Inc., where he continues to mentor the next generation of leaders.

Stenette Byrd IV is a man of two worlds: the high-speed landscape of digital innovation and the precision-driven greens of the golf course. As a student at Norfolk State University (Behold the Green and Gold),

Stenette serves as the Director of Technology and Innovation for Third Force Educational Solutions, LLC.

In his professional role, Stenette IV is the architect behind the curtain. He spearheads website development and oversees all Information Technology tasks, ensuring that the brand's digital platforms are as dynamic and user-friendly as a perfectly manicured fairway. From optimizing internal systems to implementing cutting-edge digital tools, his focus is on empowering young leaders through innovative solutions.

In addition, Stenette IV is a former high school varsity golf and soccer captain who has spent thousands of hours mastering the mechanics of the swing. While his father, Stenette Byrd III, views golf as a problem to be solved with grit and geometry, Stenette IV approaches it as an athletic flow. Whether he is troubleshooting technical issues or a "slice," Stenette IV is dedicated to helping leaders navigate the hazards of the modern world, one hole at a time.

Leadership Lessons From A Terrible Golfer

In Dr. Byrd's First Book "Leadership Lessons from a Terrible Golfer," he shows you how to get back up from a nasty fall and wants aspiring leaders and veterans alike to follow in his footsteps. Taking a candid, sometimes comic approach in retelling his experiences growing up in Hampton, Virginia, and later putting two and two together, pun intended, at Norfolk State University as a mathematics major, Dr. Byrd stresses that our setbacks are not the end, but only set us back up again for round two.

This isn't another one of those overly-hyped leadership books that only tell and don't show. Each chapter connects a common golfing blunder, like over-swinging, for example, with a critical attribute of effective leadership, such as strategic planning and execution.

If a person can improve their golf game by learning from and minimizing golfing mistakes, you can create a thriving workplace culture and overcome any curveball thrown at you by using the same approach.

So put on your polo shirt and golf hat; it's about to get tough. How else will the tough get going?

Available Now

Coming Soon Book 3 – For Kids

My Super Smart Plan for School (And Why Golf is Kinda Silly)

Abstract:

Hi! My name is Trae, and I have a secret. My dad and my brother, Ivy, spend way too much time playing golf. Like, hours and hours! They wake up super early, even on Saturdays, just to hit a tiny white ball into a little hole. I don't get it. It looks like a lot of walking and a lot of grass.

And the funny thing is, they get so serious about it! Dad gets all grumpy when his ball goes in the water. And Ivy tries to tell him all these fancy golf rules. They talk about "handicaps" and "bogies" and "playing the course as it is." Honestly, it sounds like a lot of stress for a game!

But here's my secret: even though I think golf is a little silly, I've learned some cool stuff just by listening to them. Dad says, "Ivy, you can't force a shot you don't have." And Ivy says, "Dad, just focus on the next shot!" They talk about working hard, not giving up, and not getting mad when things don't go perfectly.

I think that's true for school too! If I just keep trying my best, even when a math problem is super tricky, I can figure it out. It's like my dad hitting a bad shot – he just needs to try again on the next one. And if I spend my time learning my ABCs and 123s, instead of worrying about things I can't change (like if my pencil breaks or if it rains at recess), then I'll be super successful!

I bet if I really wanted to, I could even beat Dad and Ivy at golf. All it takes is practice and not worrying so much. But for now, I'll stick to being super smart in school. It's way more fun than chasing a little white ball!

Additional Resources

We have reached the end of our round, but the real work of leadership happens on the course every day. Use this chart to evaluate your progress. Compare these ratings to your initial Pre-Assessment (page 2) to track your development and identify your next targets for improvement.

The Scorecard: 18 Holes, 18 Lessons

1 - I have mastered this skill

2 - I'm pretty good in this area

3 - I want to be better in this area

4 - I really struggle in this area

5 - I have no idea why this is important

Hole	Chapter Title	The Leadership Attribute	Post-Assessment Score
1	The Tee Box	Vision And Setting The Tone	
2	The Trap Of The Big Stick	Discipline And Restraint	
3	The Hidden Graveyard	Strategic Agility	
4	Out of the Pit And Into The Sand	Resilience And Grit	
5	The High Stakes Of The Hazzard	Risk Management	
6	Reading The Wind	Situational Awareness	
7	The Fine Print	Attention To Detail	
8	Trampolines And Territory	Patience And Endurance	

9	The Mentor And The Mentee	Mentoring And Mentorship	
10	Seizing Opportunities	Seizing Opportunities	
11	The Sidehill Lie	Balance And Stability	
12	Divots And Decisions	Accountability And Repairing Trust	
13	The High Stakes Of The Inner Circle	People Before Programs	
14	Finesse Over Force	Emotional Intelligence	
15	Playing It Where It Lies	Leading *Your* Organization	
16	Leading Within The White Stakes	Ethics And Boundaries	
17	The Five-Foot Foundation	Performance Under Pressure	
18	Choosing the Right Team Members	Choosing The Right Team Members	
		Total Pre-Assessment Score	

Reflection(s):

Goal(s):

www.thirdforcesoulutions.com/resources

Terrible Golfer's Connection Journal: Keep The Score, Keep The Story

If there is one thing my dad and I have learned from our 18 holes of debate, laughter, and lost balls, it's this: **The scorecard tells you what you shot, but the story tells you what you learned.**

Over the years, we have shared the fairways with so many talented, brilliant, and genuinely interesting people. From seasoned educators and community leaders to fellow students and weekend warriors, every person we've played with has brought a unique perspective to the game, and to life.

Our only regret? We wish we had kept a better record of them.

That is why we created *A Terrible Golfer's Connection Journal*. This isn't just a book for tracking your birdies; it's a resource for tracking your journey. Whether you are networking for your career or building lifelong friendships, this journal ensures that the memories made between the tee box and the green aren't forgotten the moment you put your clubs in the trunk.

What's Inside? Every round of golf is an opportunity to learn something new about the person riding in the cart next to you. This log is designed to be fast, practical, and actionable—just like this book.

Each entry allows you to record:

- **The Basics:** Date and the Golf Course (so you can remember those hidden gems).
- **The Lineup:** Space for your name and the names of the players in your group.
- **The Stats:** A spot for your final score (and maybe a note on if you beat my dad).
- **The Takeaway:** A dedicated section for **Notes** to jot down a piece of advice, a funny story, or a leadership insight shared during the round.

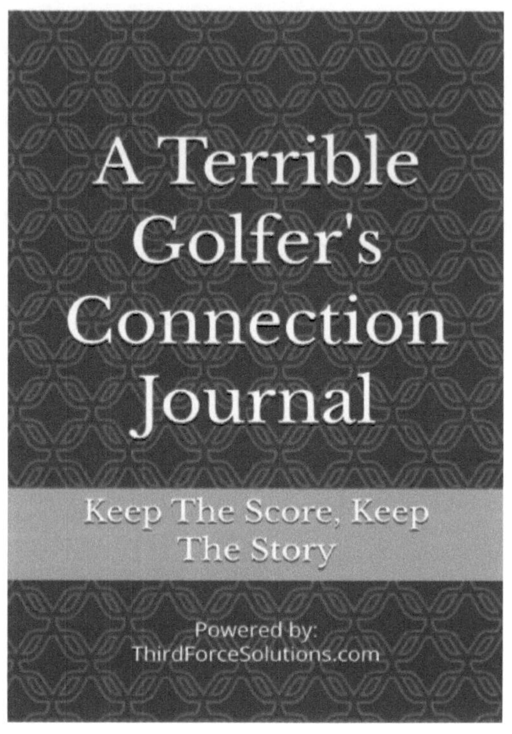

Use the QR code below to order your journal now or visit
www.thirdforcesoulutions.com/resources

Your Sample Personal Connection Log is located on the next page:

The Terrible Golfer's Connection Journal

Keep the Score, Keep the Story

Date:	Player(s)	Score(s)
Golf Course:		
Notes/Insights:		

Date:	Player(s)	Score(s)
Golf Course:		
Notes/Insights:		

Date:	Player(s)	Score(s)
Golf Course:		
Notes/Insights:		

www.ingramcontent.com/pod-product-compliance
Ingram Content Group UK Ltd.
Pitfield, Milton Keynes, MK11 3LW, UK
UKHW041641190726
13854UKWH00006B/2628